*Interface California Corporation*
*Eureka, California 95501*

# WITH
# NATURE'S
# CHILDREN

# WITH NATURE'S CHILDREN

EMMA B. FREEMAN [1880-1928] –
CAMERA AND BRUSH

BY PETER E. PALMQUIST

*For Linda*

# Table of Contents

Cover illustration . . . entitled "Out of the Past" is a hand-painted photograph from Emma B. Freeman's Northern California Indian Series.

# FAIRY FORESTS

*by Madison Cawein*

*The freckled jewel flower swings*
*Its blossoms where the orchid blushed,*
*And where the woodland deeps hang hushed*
*The rapturous veery sings.*
*The saplings crook their arms at me*
*And whisper with their leaves, "Come see*
*The wonder and the mystery*
*That haunt the heart of things."*

*And then I saw a spirit wild*
*That danced upon the waterfall,*
*And like the beauty of a child,*
*Hung laughing over all.*
*I saw the fairy of the fern*
*Toss emerald looks at every turn*
*And in the dew the elfin burn*
*That holds the rose in thrall.*
*I saw frail presences of light*
*Gleam into form and glimmer round;*
*And with them, crystalling in sight,*
*The winds with wild flowers crowned.*
*I saw dim sylvans sit at ease*
*Within the hearts of hidden trees,*
*And in the brambles, watching these,*
*The faun that none hath found.*

*I saw the music all around,*
*The lisp of leaf, the water's song,*
*Evolve a form, a shape of sound,*
*That glimmered green along.*
*I saw the happiness that fills*
*The heart of things that never stills,*
*Dance like the rapture of the rills,*
*And leap the woods among.*

*A moment more and I had seen*
*The soul itself it faery bared,*
*And all that nature's self may mean*
*To me had been declared.*
*But lo! there came a sudden lull*
*In action, and a step fell dull.*
*A mortal's, and the beautiful*
*Fled, like a wild thing, scared.*

**Humboldt Times, February 27, 1914**

# Introduction
## BY MARGERY MANN

The present volume might well be sub-titled "The Rise and Fall of Emma B. Freeman," for Emma was a heroine who would appeal to the novelist as well as to the photographic historian. She was a complex woman — attractive, lively, part shrewd business-woman, part striving artist; ambitious, yet inclined to be ruled by her caprices. Many of the women who have become professional photographers have been strong-willed, even eccentric, but few have been as flamboyantly so as Emma. Perhaps her eccentricities would have been overlooked in a city, but Emma and her husband made their home in the small town of Eureka, California; and when a married woman hopped on the train to leave town with a comparative stranger who had been the leading speaker at the visiting Chatauqua, it was front-page news.

Emma was self-taught as a photographer. She seems to have absorbed information about the medium as she worked, but she was aware of some of the conventions of her time — the decorated studio backgrounds, which she painted herself instead of buying from a supply house; the careful mounting of the prints on several papers in graduated colors to make tasteful, artistic borders. She had been trained a little as a painter, and she confused painting and photography when it suited her fancy. She used the soft-focus lenses that were then in vogue in fashionable portrait studios, and often colored her prints, but she also drew with a pencil well-defined frameworks which supported her vignetted images. Occasionally, when she had no ready-made studio background that fitted her model, she sketched something appropriate on the print itself.

Like many Californians of her time, she was fascinated by the Native Americans. They were the only contact this romantic woman had ever had with an exotic culture, and she photographed them in contrived settings and poses that were more suited to a dream world than to the harsh reality of their lives. Her photographs were sympathetic, perhaps because her subjects were outsiders in the small town of Eureka because of their race, and she too was an outsider because of her capriciousness, her independence, and her artistic yearnings.

She was ambitious and resourceful. She studied the magazines to see which ones published photographs, and her Native American portraits appeared in several California and national publications. She seems to have had no contact with artist photographers of the San Francisco Bay Area, although we have one bit of evidence that she must have known of their existence. *Camera Craft* was the leading West Coast photography magazine for the first forty years of the Twentieth century, and it was full of tips and hints and how-to-do-it articles which Emma, like most other California photographers, read to improve their techniques. An article about Emma appeared in *Camera Craft* in May, 1917, *"An Artist with the Camera,"* by a writer with the unlikely name of N. A. Wog. It was the only time Emma was mentioned, and Wog surfaced in the pages of *Camera Craft* for only the one article, a glorious hymn of praise to the talent of a young artist who had sprung from unpromising beginnings in rural Nebraska. Can anyone doubt that N. A. Wog was in reality Emma B. Freeman? One wonders where she got the name.

**Margery Mann**
Davis, California

# Preface

I first encountered Emma Freeman's work among the heirlooms in a local Victorian home, where for a few contented hours I had settled down to review a fine assortment of old family pictures — in bundles, boxes and albums. While examining a pile of oversized photographs, I retrieved two folio folders. Each contained a striking Indian portrait, the first entitled "Twilight Meditation," the second "Ah-Pura-Ah-Way." Clearly visible in the lower corner of each print was the bold signature: "Emma B. Freeman."

As a collector of regional photographica, I was familiar with the Freeman Art Company label — to which Emma would be linked — and had already gathered over fifty commercial examples; fraternal and family groups, street and waterfront scenes, portraits, and numerous photo-postcards. But these artistically-conceived photographs were a revelation; their very presence demanded an explanation of their origin.

Casting about for information on Emma B. Freeman and her romantic imagery, I learned that specimens of her work, while uncommon and widely scattered, were not rare. Moreover, Emma herself was not unknown, though her images had become so dispersed they were no longer recognized as part of a much larger pictorial statement. As these pictures resurfaced and the first few details of her life came to light, it became obvious that Emma's lifestyle and her artistic efforts in rural Northern California would be interesting to resolve.

Emma was intriguing on many counts. She was a woman artist in a male-dominated cultural backwater. Her lifestyle was independent and unconventional, atypical in the early years of this century. The Native Americans she befriended and recorded were but a generation removed from their original culture. But the qualities which truly distinguished her — and which have made this project so personally involving — were her extraordinary and complex need for self-expression, and her sheer determination to fulfill her creative goals. To this day she epitomizes the ceaseless pursuit of an inner vision.

Researching her life has been challenging partly because Emma lived at a time which is now at the edge of living memory. A number of people still remember her, but few can provide insight into her feelings and aspirations. Mostly it is the rumor and gossip which have survived the intervening years. Historical documentation has answered some questions, but raised others. In many ways Emma remains an enigmatic figure.

I have lived in Humboldt County, California since 1945, and have practiced photography in the same geographic region as Emma for nearly 25 years. From this background I hoped to understand the social and professional problems which confronted her. In the end, I found no little difficulty in explaining the sociology of unfolding events. Perhaps my efforts are presumptuous: I am not a woman, a painter, an Indian, or even an historian. At best, I hope to share with the reader my increasing surprise and admiration as I retraced, as best I could, the life of a most remarkable person.

Although her Indian portraits and stylized images of women form the body of work for which Emma wished to be known — and the only photographs which she signed — she also produced a large output of commercial photography which is poorly represented in this monograph. To a great degree, most examples of Emma's painting, drawing, and handcrafts have eluded my search, victims of time and change. However the hand-painted photograph which appears on the cover of this book attests to her skill with the brush.

I have included two appendices and a catalogue of Native American images for those who may wish a fuller understanding of Emma's milieu. The first explores social attitudes towards women's rights and the arts during her years in Eureka. The second deals with the historical interaction of Northern California's Native Americans with the newly-entrenched white society, a process in which Emma's Indian portraits had some influence.

The catalogue contains those Native American images which are thus far attributable to Emma B. Freeman. The images, titles and information given should serve as a guide to the subject and do not represent the total output of her work in this area. The Newberry Library in Chicago and the California State Library represent the major public repositories of Freeman Native American imagery known to the author at this time. Although the Newberry's is the most extensive collection it is also the poorer representative sample of her best efforts, the most beautifully prepared examples are at the California State Library or in private holdings.

Again, it should be stressed that this catalogue represents only one aspect of her work. Moreover many examples represented in this group are, I feel, culled from the overall preparation of her Northern California and Indian Head series of Native American portraits. At the time of the preparation of this catalogue it is my feeling that many other examples from this series have not been available to me. Therefore the catalogue serves as a starting point to which other intelligence may be added.

Anthropologists should not expect new and significant insights from Emma's photographs. She recognized two basic tribal distinctions: the Klamath, which included all those with family ties which originated in the region adjacent to the Klamath River from its mouth to the town of Orleans; and the Hoopa, those from the Hoopa Indian reservation. Additionally, Emma placed artistic considerations before those of traditional accuracy in terms of dress and behavior. For example, women of the Hupa (Hoopa) tribal family did not utilize either a headband or wear a feather in their hair.

Lastly, there have been a number of unexpected and so far unresolved examples of Freeman Art Company images which are intriguing and have not been satisfactorily classified. An example of this is typified by the discovery, in Eureka, of glass plate negatives labeled by the Freeman Art Company which picture the construction of the Panama Canal.

My most pleasant personal experience during the course of this project has been the hours spent with Bertha Stevens Chamley at her home in Eureka. With quiet chuckles and twinkling eye she recalled her years as Emma's close friend.

Margery Mann has provided the crucial vote of confidence I needed to complete this study. Whether she is aware of it or not, her encouragement has proved invaluable.

I should also like to express my appreciation to Robert and Genelle Dolezal and the staff of Interface California Corporation for

Subjectively the painter and the photographer stretch after the same goal. Technically they approach it from opposite directions. The painter starts with a bare surface and creates detail, the photographer is supplied therewith.

(Henry R. Poore, Pictorial Composition; and the critical judgement of pictures)

15

their editorial assistance; Marilyn Andrews, Susan Bevier, Sidney Dominitz, Lincoln Kilian, Erich Schimps, Debbra Walters, William Johnson of the Hoopa Tribal Museum, Kim Yerton and Frances Purser of the Indian Action Library for research and manuscript assistance: F. Peter Weil and the staff of the Newberry Library, Thérèse Lawrence and Kenneth I. Pettitt of the California State Library, and Allan R. Carlson for their kind assistance in making Freeman imagery available for this project. Any errors in the final version are, of course, my own.

**Peter E. Palmquist**
Arcata, California

# Chronology

Emma B. Freeman, like the half-Indian, half-white subjects in her romanticized photographs of Native Americans, was caught frequently between two worlds. Ultimately her art, and her strength, lay in the manner in which she combined the best elements of both.

She was a renegade woman who defied the constraints of the male-dominated world of the early 1900's. She was a photographer intent not on realism but on poetry. She craved artistic recognition but chose to live much of her life in a cultural backwater, a white taking pictures of Indians.

Derided as a Bohemian by small-town society, she made her studio a salon for outcasts. Though keen on social acceptance, she courted scandal and a subsequent adultery suit by having a highly publicized fling with an ex-governor of Illinois. Her intimate friends knew her as "Toots."

As a photographer, she wavered between the extremes of artistic pretension and hard-headed photojournalism. The Indian photographs of Emma Freeman do **not** document the Native American heritage in faithful detail. Instead they express her idealized notions of the Indian as the embodiment of the mysteries of nature. Yet, during World War One, her pluck and daring while photographing a naval disaster off the California coast won her fame as an authentic journalist and earned her the title of "Official Government Photographer."

Her series of Indian portraits remains her most noteworthy achievement. But these photographs grew from her probable misconceptions regarding the Indian's oneness with the universe and her own deep-seated need to identify with nature. Even nature sometimes proved inadequate for her — so she painted wilderness backdrops for her studio and, on at least one occasion, used a blond European model to pose as an Indian brave.

Emma came to photography relatively late in life, long after her formal training as a painter. In all likelihood this accounted for her efforts to forge a synthesis of the two disciplines — painting and photography. Indeed, she considered herself an artist employing camera and brush, and signed her hand-colored or retouched photographs as a painter would a canvas.

At the same time that she was proving herself an astute businesswoman and struggling to artistically reconcile photography and painting, she was romantically focusing on a neglected people — the Native Americans — who had been subjected to virtual genocide only a generation before.

In an article in *Pacific Outdoors* magazine in 1917, Emma displayed her spiritual attachment to nature and her reverence for the Indian. She referred to the Indians as "Nature's monarchs of the wild," portrayed their life as "heroic and romantic," and inveighed against encroaching civilization and blood-mingling for effacing traditional customs and crafts.

To Emma a visit to the Indian areas of Northwestern California produced this reaction:

*. . . it fills one with the wild free spirit of the plain, the lake and the forest, expands one's lungs and vision at the same time and forms the basis of a wider, higher appreciation of God's great universe in its primitive and most beautiful phase.*

**(Pacific Outdoors, October 1917)**

Similarly, in a comment in the same article on the subjects of her stylized portraits, Emma betrayed a well-meant bias when she wrote: *"However the Indian, with his natural grace, makes an ideal model. He has none of the artful and annoying lack of control of facial expression and has no desire to appear to be other than his natural self, a weakness of his white brother and sister."*

Emma, a self-taught photographer of a strange people in an awesome land, had traveled a long way from the flat plains of rural Nebraska. Little is known of her early life except that she was born Emma Belle Richart in 1880, on a farmland homestead, to William

(photograph opposite) Emma's most often reproduced self-image. Note the pencil enhancement and signature, circa 1914.

18

Emma B. Freeman - Northern California Indian and Scenic Artist. Eureka. Cal.
—Camera and Brush—

19

K. Richart and Belle (Zoover) Richart, transplanted Ohioans and presumably of German stock.

The best insight into her early years came from Emma herself when she described her own youth and aspirations in an article published in 1917.

*That "artists are born and not made" is surely demonstrated by Emma B. Freeman, for while it was the dream of a little eight-year-old, pigtailed, Nebraska girl, that "someday" she would be a real artist; a farm in the middle West during the "lean" years cannot, by any stretch of the imagination, be considered a desirable environment for the birth, nourishment and development of artistic tendencies. But from the time "little Emma" found that Nebraska clay could be fashioned into figures other than mud pies, and when her earliest artistic effort, drawing "teacher" on the blackboard, earned her fame among her schoolmates and a spanking from her subject, every moment that could be stolen from study and the never ending task of "helping mother" was consecrated to drawing pictures and coloring them with crayons, a ten-cent box of which was her first and greatly prized possession in the way of artist's materials.*

*In early womanhood the starved and narrow existence incidental to chaperoning cows, pigs and chickens on the homestead, became unbearable to a nature that thrilled with high ideals and a love for the beautiful. Possessed of a spark of artistic talent that would not be smothered, in the face of warnings of friends and entreaties of relatives, a pilgrimage was planned to San Francisco where the little farm girl had ever dreamed lay fame and fortune.*

*Emma's carefully saved "egg money" fund was soon depleted in buying an outfit for the journey, and for purely economic reasons a ticket was purchased to Denver only. There a rapidly thinning purse necessitated a flight to a haven of refuge behind the ribbon counter of a department store, where a weekly pittance of six dollars was soon augmented by the manufacture and sale of flowers fashioned from ribbon and the occasional sale of a sketch to a friendly art dealer.*

**(Camera Craft, May 1917)**

This account of humble beginnings and artistic yearnings went on to stress her ambitions and subsequent success. Further memories of her family and birthplace appear to have been effectively erased with Emma's purchase of a ticket to Denver.

It was in Denver that Emma met the man who was to be her husband for 13 years. It was the turn of the century, and Denver — whose 130,000 people knew it as the "Queen City of the West" — was a busy railroad axis for the extensive mining and livestock industries of the surrounding countryside.

Edwin Ruthven Freeman was among those attracted to the bustling city from the small town of Greeley, located some 60 miles to the north. The 22-year old Freeman had been employed in various occupations before becoming a salesman for the prosperous garment industry. In this capacity he traveled widely, making his rounds of the various department and dry-goods stores throughout the greater Denver area. Edwin is remembered as a handsome, personable young man, who was greatly taken by the attractive young saleslady he met on one of his selling trips. He began making a point of visiting her whenever possible. Emma was intrigued by Edwin's widespread knowledge and freestyle traveling life. Within a few months she came to view Edwin as her one chance to escape the suffocating existence of a ribbon clerk. The two were married on the 26th of November, 1902.

As a couple, Edwin and Emma Freeman appeared to present the epitome of attractiveness. Emma was blue-eyed, petite and of slender build, with dark hair prematurely streaked with grey. Edwin was tall, forceful, and capable; while Emma was filled with an ambition to acquire worldly knowledge and gain personal recognition. These very traits would become, in the years ahead, part of the forces that divided them.

For the present, however, they were content. The Freemans soon left Denver. Ed's savings and occasional employment enroute finally brought them to Emma's childhood goal, San Francisco. For Emma, San Francisco marked the first step on her path to achievement. However, like many others before her, she soon found that it was not easy to subsist through artistic pretension. San Francisco, nearly three times the size of Denver, presented an overwhelming experience to a farmgirl so recently from Nebraska. Ed found a succession of different jobs. By 1904, he was doing very well as a salesman for the prestigious Market Street firm of S. N. Wood & Company, merchant tailors and clothiers. To supplement their income, Emma also worked outside of their home. Her mornings were spent soliciting orders for the hand-crafted curios that she prepared and delivered on commission to her clients in the afternoon. Among her stocks-in-trade were leather novelties, burnt wood gee-gaws, painted Easter and Christmas items, hand-colored photographs, and sketches in both pastels and watercolors.

The Freemans finally saved enough money to open a tiny shop at the corner of Octavia and Union Streets. Although principally a stationer's, in time their shop sold a variety of items. Emma began marketing her own handcrafts directly to the public. As money became less tight, she began to extend a creative expression to her efforts. She felt that now was the time to make her childhood dream a reality . . . time to become a true artist.

Emma had begun to 'expand her circle of acquaintances in the strange city, meeting a number of aspiring young artists and students. Acting on their advice, she enrolled in a well-established art studio on Post Street. Her teacher was Giuseppe Cadenasso, a noted San Francisco landscape painter. A modest man with many friends and a sizeable following of students, Cadenasso quickly became an important part of Emma's life. She religiously attended his classes. Encouraged by her instructor, Emma polished and honed her skills at drawing and painting.

The contacts and shared interests of this period formed a vital link towards self-understanding, and her spirits soared. Spurring her attentiveness was her desire for public recognition of her efforts as fine art. Throughout the years that followed, Emma maintained a relationship with several of the artists of this period, and she often visited Cadenasso at his studio until his death in 1918.

With both of the Freemans working hard, the shop prospered and their long-term prospects appeared bright. Then, on April 18, 1906, the disastrous San Francisco earthquake and its consequent fires destroyed their shop. The Freemans like thousands of others were forced to flee San Francisco. For Emma these events were a bitter interruption of her march toward achievement.

The earthquake also damaged Cadenasso's Post Street studio, causing him to relocate in the Russian Hill area of San Francisco. A revealing glimpse of his new facility, which Emma knew very well, is provided in the following excerpt from an article entitled, *"A visit to the picturesque hillside studio of Giuseppe Cadenasso."*

*I soon found myself at the entrance to the studio and in the presence of the genius who presides over it.*

*There was something strangely antique, something reminiscent of an old curiosity shop, something strangely melancholy in the atmosphere of the interior of the dimly lighted studio, with its ancient hangings and its furniture . . . A large window afforded a splendid view of the bay, discernible now, however, only because of the flickering electric lights which grew dimmer and dimmer through the gathering mists. The searchlight on lonely Alcatraz Island was throwing its restless glances in all directions, while the dismal wail of the foghorn penetrated the evening stillness with ominous warning. And there were those lovely, lovely canvases before me!*

(California's Magazine, 1916)

Emma also remembered the effects of this disaster:

*Then came the San Francisco fire and a fresh start on a borrowed hundred dollars capital in the city of Eureka. There the little San Francisco art shop was duplicated . . .*

(Camera Craft, May 1917)

One can only speculate on the origin of the Freemans' decision to relocate in the obscure little city of Eureka, nearly 300 miles north of San Francisco.

Its surrounding countryside may have appealed to an individual like Ed, who was intrigued by oft-repeated stories of giant trees and strong men. Emma, by comparison, must have been shattered by the loss of contacts from her business and art acquaintances, and by the ignominious retreat from San Francisco.

At the time the Freemans arrived in the Northern California seacoast town, it was still Edwin who made the important family decisions. Ed most likely was the one who borrowed the money necessary for a new start, and probably selected the site of their relocation in the Humboldt County region.

The county itself is over 100 miles long, averaging a width of 35 miles. It has a total land area of 3,573 square miles, roughly equal to the combined areas of Delaware and Rhode Island. Its northern boundary is only 50 miles from Oregon, and approximately eighty-five percent of the region is coastal mountain terrain mantled by luxurious forests. Large stands of giant redwood trees grow within the county, and numerous streams have formed flood plains near its central coast. The climate is moderate but considerable precipitation falls from October through April. Eureka, the county seat and most populous city, is sited on beautiful and economically significant Humboldt Bay.

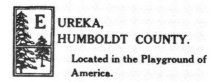

In 1907, Eureka still echoed its frontier tradition. It was active and vital, and most certainly a masculine community. Founded in 1853, it was known principally for the harvesting and milling of giant redwood trees. Eureka was also an important shipping and service port for the vast inland mountainous areas of Northern California. It boasted a population of nearly 8,000, including more than 2,000 of foreign extraction. Eureka's Indian population was not usually enumerated, while its Chinese inhabitants had been forced to flee the city in 1885 and again in 1906. By comparison with the cosmopolitanism of San Francisco, Eureka was a cultural backwater. Social activities were limited to recitals and dances, fraternal activities, and Sunday music in the city park — usually featuring the local marching band. In addition to these activities, an early form of motion picture films were shown every evening at the Cineograph Theatre. Two legitimate theatres, the Ingomar and the Margarita, rounded out the city's offerings. In these houses, as many as two stage productions per week drew crowds that paid a 25 to 50-cent admission. During the 1907 season a cultural highpoint was reached when an opera was presented.

In the area of fine art, however, Eureka was practically a wasteland. Emma was again reduced to producing minor commissions and novelties, while Edwin worked at a progression of unrewarding jobs. Then, perceiving a need for a competent source of art goods, Ed put his sales experience to work. Using their small home as a base for operations, they shared the effort of rebuilding their finances and establishing new contacts.

As they worked together, however, several differences emerged. While living in a metropolitan area such as San Francisco, with its diversity of social opportunity, there had been activities and stimulation for both Ed and Emma. Rural Humboldt County provided little such stimulation. As a man, Edwin could move freely through local society, with potential access to all levels of commerce. As a woman, particularly in Eureka, Emma was bound by traditions to conform to accepted norms of wifehood in a small-town society. Her distant origin, upbringing, and lack of identifiable family ties provided cause for discrimination. It was also considered unusual for a woman to attempt employment in a role that brought attention to herself as a creative individual.

Professional artists verged, for the most part, on the precipitous edge of Bohemian existence, and were not welcome in many parts of

Eureka's society. Emma Freeman might well have withdrawn from this hostile environment, but she went on to win acceptance.

In the meantime, Ed's affection for Eureka grew. He was a good conversationalist and quickly established a reputation among the other young men of the town as a "fine fellow." He became acquainted with the Seely brothers, who, in addition to being members of a vocal quartet, had taken up commercial photography. Ed became fascinated by the potential of photography and quickly learned the business by working for the Seelys' studio part-time. Ed Freeman's growing career in photography suited him well; however, his photographic excursions drew him away from Eureka with increasing frequency. Buoyed by his easy acceptance in a male-dominated world, he became technically proficient as a photographer and was filled with confidence. Ironically, these advances in his career were accomplished at the expense of his relationship with Emma, who felt thwarted by her inability to achieve recognition for her own creativity. She became determined not to ride to success on her husband's shirttails.

It should be noted that Emma did not perceive herself as a radical, nor was her attitude based on what has come to be described as women's rights. She did, however, identify with many features of feminism, and fully understood the constraints placed upon women by small-town society (see appendix A).

Emma did not seek to dominate her husband. Rather, she worked diligently to achieve artistic and emotional independence while granting Edwin freedom to proceed in the matters of importance to him. Their marriage remained childless.

Despite their growing difficulties, the Freemans — by working together — multiplied their savings. By 1908, they were able to move their fledgling business from their home to a downtown commercial location. Known as the Freeman Art Company, this enterprise was the first of several rapidly expanding business locations in Eureka.

Despite the success of their business enterprise the Freemans were not content. In January, 1909, The *Eureka Herald* announced, *"Freeman Art Company to quit business."* The notice cited Mrs. Freeman's general health and her desire to return to San Francisco to renew her art studies as contributory factors. This event appears to signal the emotional low point of Emma's sojourn in Eureka. It is unclear as to the reasons why the Freemans did not depart as planned. Subsequent notices concerning the Freemans indicate a strong determination to succeed within the local business community.

Eventually the shop was located on a busy thoroughfare that served as the area's north/south highway. Their business offered a wide range of novelties and art supplies. Eureka had only recently been connected with San Francisco by an overland road, and motorcars shortened the distances even more. The automobile brought an ever-increasing number of visitors who desired souvenirs of the beautiful area. The Freemans eventually expanded into an adjacent shop with large glass display-windows that enabled them to intrigue the passerby. The Pillsbury Picture Company, a specialist in panoramic photographs of California's scenic areas, successfully marketed their line through the Freeman Art Company. A. C. Pillsbury, president of the company, commented in a letter to the Freemans, *"Eureka, under your handling has proven one of our best customers . . . you may be interested to hear that one of the pictures called 'Rays of Sunshine in the Redwoods' has proven one of our most valuable views and is selling readily all over California."* Since panoramas had proved to be so popular, Ed worked diligently to become sufficiently skilled so that the store could offer scenic views of his own making. By 1910, he was achieving considerable success in all aspects of commercial photography.

Although other Eureka establishments, including stationers, carried lines of art goods, the Freeman Art Company also provided detailed information about the proper use of their merchandise. Those with advanced knowledge often stopped by to engage in shop talk, a pastime in which Emma was always willing to participate. As the success of the enterprise grew, so did Emma's responsibility for the day-by-day operation of the store. In spite of the increasing burden, she stole time to interact with the few professional artists of the area. She also continued her formal painting lessons with Charles Harmon, an established artist, who made a number of brief appearances in Eureka. Harmon had once resided in Denver, but now made San Jose, California his permanent home. Skilled at western landscapes, he was a well-regarded craftsman. Included among his commissions were at least eighteen from the Santa Fe Railroad Company. Harmon, who loved to paint the giant redwood trees, encouraged Emma and they became good friends.

Emma's willingness to expend more than the needed amount of effort at a task frequently ensured accomplishment. Such attention to her work might easily have caused her to neglect the development of friendships. Such was not the case, for she enjoyed people. To distinguish her from Ed's maiden sister, Emma Freeman, she was usually called Emma B. To particularly close friends, however, she was playfully known as "Toots." Her manner was charming, and she met the public effectively, but did not escape all gossip and criticism. Eureka's society must have viewed her efforts with amused tolerance, likely thinking her pretentious and Bohemian. Perhaps it was the result of this prevailing view that caused Emma to attract others whose nature could be construed as similarly unconventional.

Freeman Art Company, 5th and H Street location. B. P. O. E. (Elks) convention in progress, September 6, 1915.

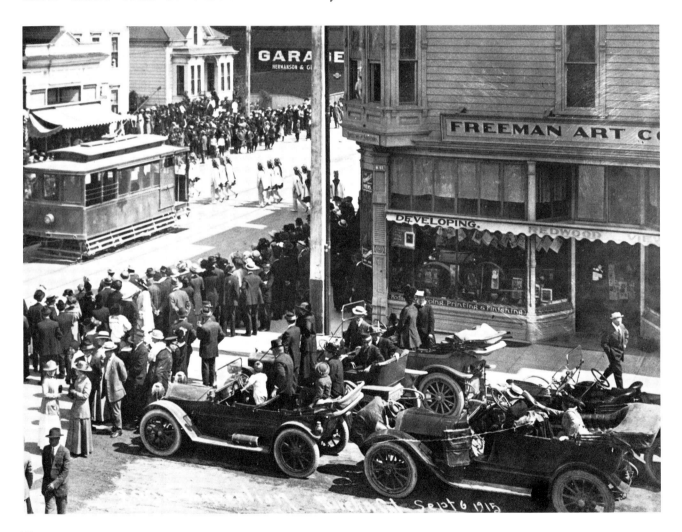

Emma's personal friendships were generally strong, and often separate from her daily business relationships.

Taken as a social phenomenon, the Freeman Art Company provided a unique entry into the local business community. Not strictly an art gallery, it served the dual function of a gift shop for those looking for a clever handmade souvenir and a supply house for those in need of a new paintbrush. Quickly extending its influence beyond these functions, however, the shop began to act as an arbiter of artistic taste. In the field of photography, Edwin's scenic views competed favorably with a half-dozen other local studios. Over the years, paintings and drawings of the region were selected for sale in the Freemans' store from a small but expanding group of local painters. These artists formed a minor school of western art suited to and expressive of their isolated Northcoast habitat. Among these works, redwood and coastal landscapes predominated. While they were never destined to become widely recognized artists, C. T. Wilson, Martella Lane, Cora Wright and others joined with visitor Charles Harmon to exhibit an artistic output easily associated with the region.

In January 1910, the Freemans purchased the camera and studio equipment of Eureka photographer J. A. Meiser. Emma began at once to experiment with this equipment, exploring the possibilities of artistic portraiture. From this meager starting point, photography became her principal interest. As Emma's interview later recounted it:

*... the* [Freeman Art] *business met with varying success until the owner of a rather dilapidated photographic studio induced Mrs. Freeman to purchase his outfit. With this, but without the slightest knowledge of photography, this nervy little woman worked day and night to make the best of what she then thought was a very bad bargain.*

(Camera Craft, May 1917)

Emma's romantic, artistically-conceived portraits were destined to become very popular, especially among those interested in obtaining fashionable images of themselves. Although portraiture soon became her major emphasis, Emma also photographed many of the more exciting daily activities of Eureka and its environs. In July 1911, writer Jack London and his wife Charmian arrived in Eureka on their way to Oregon and were photographed by Emma. The Londons'

(photograph Opposite) Emma achieved considerable renown for her tableaux settings for the portraiture of women. The 3-quarter length pose is the most typical, usually coupled with studio props that were meant to approximate a home environment. She signed these examples directly on the print which differentiates these "Artistic Portraits" from the standard commercial line of portraiture.

29

mode of conveyance was a double-seated spring wagon drawn by four horses. Later immortalized by London's short story *"Navigating Four Horses North of the Bay,"* their visit was typical of the special occasions that Emma felt were worthy of her interest.

With her artistic tools now firmly in hand, Emma decided to capitalize on her considerable distance from other art centers by developing a mode of personal expression that would be both distinctive and practical. Her new self-concept was that of an artist "on the edge of nature's own wilderness." It was a romantic notion that expressed a freedom to ascend to her goal of artistic recognition. It also represented an escape from the routine of daily life into a fantasy-bordered reality of her own making. At the same time Emma perceived an awakening national interest in the exotic aspects of

Today, examples of Emma's romantic landscapes are difficult to find since they seem to have been made in a brief period during 1913-14. Later landscapes are of a more commercial nature and are not easily distinguished from the work of her assistant Fred Chamley.

nature which also interested her. With increasing sureness, Emma proceeded to identify the experiences and relationships that would strengthen her chances of achieving her creative goals.

Considered as a whole, her observations were largely romantic musings . . . a spiritual concept of nature as the common source of perfection. Mankind, especially the Native American, appeared in this idyllic paradise in roles of heroic splendor. By 1913, the popular idea of nature had begun to assume a new meaning to whole generations of young people who had never participated in the early settlers' struggle to push back the forests.

Overnight, poems with such titles as *"Faery Forests," "The Call of the Land,"* and *"Sylvan Glade"* became popular features in the local press. Other stories of the period featured such accounts as, *"NATURE MAN GOES INTO WOODS . . . will enter woods absolutely naked and without weapons and make his own living and clothes."* In direct contrast were other reports of the wilderness: *"LOS ANGELES HUNTERS GET SIX BEARS AND TWO BIG PANTHERS IN HUMBOLDT COUNTY WILDS, CITY NIMRODS ARE ENTHUSIASTIC OVER BIG GAME . . ."* Simultaneously with these events, female participation in social and civic causes became more acceptable through the formation of local women's organizations. It had become a time for causes and banners . . . not the least of which, in this land of timber and sawmills, was, *"Woodsman, spare that tree."*

Ed and Emma's relationship had, by this time, become that of two people who worked side by side, but without a shared understanding of goals. Increasingly, Edwin withdrew on traveling assignments or camping trips with his friends. He dearly loved the outdoors and the camaraderie of its fellowship. Feeling frustrated and alone, Emma moved most of her personal belongings into the store. For most of the ensuing years she would continue to reside there.

Even as the rift between Edwin and Emma widened, an event loomed which was to have a profound influence on the couple. A long period of intensive planning led, in June 1913, to the presentation of Eureka's first Chautauqua. The nationally popular concept of a Chautauqua gathering had grown out of a series of Sunday school programs that were held annually on the banks of Lake Chautauqua, New York, beginning in 1874. An adult educational institute soon evolved beyond the original program's format, combining education, recreation, and religion. By the early 1900's it had grown into a commercial enterprise. Traveling Chautauquas were held throughout the country during the summer months. The Eureka version, featuring the noted lecturer and ex-governor of Illinois, Richard B. Yates, included a week-long program of music and oratory. From the beginning Ed Freeman had participated in the planning and material arrangements for the upcoming festivities. He was also a shareholder in the Chautauqua Corporation which was formed to fund the event. Both Ed and Emma became very friendly with ex-Governor Yates during the opening period of the Chautauqua. Yates had been scheduled to speak to a large holiday crowd on the final day of the Chautauqua, on the topic *"God's Providence in American History."* Eureka dailies later described Yates as an *"exceedingly interesting speaker,"* who *"enthralled his audience."*

The events of the following morning were destined to "enthrall" an even larger audience, including people from both California and Illinois. At 8 a. m., as Yates prepared to depart Northern California, he telephoned the Freemans to join him for breakfast and to see him off on the train. A short time later the *Humboldt Times* reported his subsequent actions under the banner headline: *"EX-GOVERNOR YATES AND MRS. FREEMAN DISAPPEAR,"*

*At the depot the group* [of wellwishers] *stood talking a few minutes before the train departed and Freeman says, Yates suddenly suggested that, "You had better accompany me to the end of the line, little one" referring to his wife. . . . Mrs. Freeman* [immediately] *accepted without consulting her husband and Yates is said to have rushed to the wicket and purchased her a ticket . . .*

**(Humboldt Times, July 3, 1913)**

Emma's departure without trunk or handbag was seized upon by the newswriters, and for more than a week the scandal raged. Headlines contradicted one another: *"SAYS WIFE LEFT WITH EX-GOVERNOR YATES"; "MRS. FREEMAN DECLARES HUSBAND KNEW SHE WAS PLANNING ON A TRIP SOUTH"; "FREEMAN DECLARES WIFE TOOK TRIP WITHOUT HIS KNOWLEDGE OR CONSENT."* Newsmen pursued the participants wherever they could be found. They interviewed Ed Freeman in Eureka, Mrs. Yates in Springfield, Illinois, Ex-Governor Yates in Wisconsin (where he had gone for his next speaking engagement) and Emma in San Francisco.

The *Eureka Herald*, a local newspaper that had been scooped by the *Humboldt Times* at the onset of the story, rushed to press with the text of a telegram that purported to prove that Yates had gone straight to Illinois instead of stopping in San Francisco. Rival dailies soon determined that such speedy progress across the country was impossible in the time specified by the telegram, and branded it a fake. The best facts available today indicate that Emma Freeman and Yates arrived in San Francisco on the 11 a. m. train, had lunch together in a downtown cafe, then separated, with Yates departing for Chicago at 4 p. m.

It was characteristic of Emma that, in the uproar that attended her sudden departure to San Francisco with Yates, she retained her usual composure. Shortly after her arrival in San Francisco, she posted the following letter to her husband.

*My Dear Edwin:*

*I mailed you a card yesterday and I am now going to write. I am enjoying myself immensely, simply having the time of my life and have enjoyed every mile of my trip. Just can't begin to tell you how very much I enjoyed same, only it is rather embarrassing to be without a suitcase, but it bothered the hotel clerk more than it did me, so I relieved his mind, I told him my baggage had gone on ahead — Ha! Ha! Ha! I landed at Mrs. [Pearl] Steinau's and she hasn't gotten over laughing at my sudden arrival here, but everything is turning my way as I found a gold ring on my way up, and that is good luck, you know. I feel that I am sort of lucky that way. I found Mr. Yates a most charming companion.*

*When I got to the end of the RR Route,* [the train only went part way and the middle portion of the trip was by automobile stage] *I spoke to Mrs. Smythe and told her I would like to go on and that I would take advantage of Mr. Smythe's* [the stage driver] *invitation to go down and she said sure that would be OK, so it didn't cost me to ride on the auto. I met Mr. S at Bell Springs and he told me to keep on and when I returned, to plan on staying a few days at the camp with them, so I gladly accepted his invitation and will join the autos to Young's and shall stay a few days and then return home.*

*At 11 a. m., July 4 — Pearl and I will view the military parade from Van Ness Ave. There will be 5,000 uniformed men and it was for this* [that] *I wanted to stay over the 4th. At 2 p. m. we will go to the G. G. Park to listen to Samuel M. Shortridge and at 8 p. m. at Mission Park near our home, — band concert and fireworks.*

33

## UNSCRAMBLING YATES

There was a young man named Yates
Who once got mixed in his dates,
    But a long-distance wire
    Proclaimed all a liar
Who doubted his wonderful gaits.

So an editor made his defense
Without any just recompense:
    "He was here in a dash,
    Over there like a flash,
According to urgent events."

This lecturer had a good wife
who helped him in case of strife,
    As she too was Yates
    She unscrambled the dates
When many inquires were rife.

And the paper of notarial fame
Now denies any particle of blame
    For the mixing of dates
    Affecting young Yates
Or rumors concerning the same.

(Humboldt Times, July 23, 1913)

*I am enjoying the city — we went to the Court [theatre] and saw "Everywoman" which was a grand play — and every woman ought to see it. I do hope you won't worry about me, as I can assure you that I am OK and have one blank check of [the] Humboldt Co. Bank, and I am going to draw today on my own account.*

*Yesterday, she [Mrs. Steinau] and I visited Mr. Cadenasso at his studio and met Mrs. C. Mrs. S found her very charming and interesting as they are both musical and their boy is studying oratory and he kindly volunteered to recite for us and in turn I gave "Daseo". Mr. C. is just the same artistic character, full of emotion and she is less careworn as she has taken up Christian Science, so to sum it all up, we enjoyed the afternoon. Today we will go downtown and look at all the pretty things.*

*Will close and Pearl joins me in sending you her love and best wishes, and give Mary [Steinhauer] my love.*

*As ever your loving, toots.*

(Correspondence, July 3, 1913)

By the time Emma's chatty letter arrived in Eureka, the fury of the scandal was reaching its peak. Edwin was furious. He had appeared ridiculous in the eyes of many of the townspeople, and in response had his attorney meet Emma upon her return to Eureka. The outcome of this confrontation was a permanent separation. The legal procedure of the day required at least a one-year separation before divorce was possible. The terms of the separation included a division of property. Edwin received all assets such as their jointly held stock shares and a parcel of land in San Mateo County. Emma retained the proprietorship of the Freeman Art Company. Emma's great strength of purpose was again revealed, for, in light of what amounted to a severe censure of her actions, she immediately returned to her everyday life without apparent guilt or trepidation. Ed, by comparison, appeared devastated by the exposure of their marital differences, which was to lead to their divorce two years later.

In the spring of 1915, Ed sued Emma under the adultery clause of their separation agreement. Filed by a newly-formed law firm comprised of Ed's personal friends, the suit detailed a series of charges and allegations that were duly reported in the daily newspapers. This coverage again threw Emma and Edwin into the spotlight of public opinion.

The suit's principal charges concerned the episode of two years before, adding a second accusation of unfaithfulness involving a Richard Seeley. Emma selected a long-established law firm to represent her, and called upon her close friends for support and counsel. Among her confidantes was Mary (Minnie) Steinhauer, who had successfully divorced her own husband earlier.

The divorce transcripts are lengthy, and many parts seem sensational even 60 years later. Emma calmly denied each charge. Mixing the sublime with the ridiculous, less salacious passages such as the following, part of the sixth interrogatory, probably brought a smile to the faces of many of the participants:

**Q.** *Did the said Richard Yates on the June 30, 1913, and while on the automobile stage between McCann and Longvale exchange embraces at every bridge and culvert crossed by said automobile stage on said trip, with said Emma B. Freeman?*

Later in the proceedings, Pearl Steinau (Emma's San Francisco friend) was called as a witness for the defendant, and her responses to Edwin's lawyer undoubtedly increased those smiles to outright laughter:

**Q.** *Did Mrs. Freeman say anything to you about kissing with Mr. Yates?*
**A.** *Yes, I believe she did mention it.*
**Q.** *Now, what did they say about it?*
**A.** *Just merely that she kissed him or he her.*
**Q.** *Did she say anything about being kissed as they passed through each tunnel?*
**A.** *I think so. She mentioned something about a tunnel.*
**Q.** *Isn't it a fact, Mrs. Steinau, that she decided to come to San Francisco after Mr. Yates first kissed her?*
**A.** *She might possibly have said something like that, but I considered it a joke.*
**Q.** *But did she say it?*
**A.** *She was so full of fun and joking that I did not pay much attention to what she did say.*

(**Divorce transcripts, Edwin R. Freeman**
**vs Emma B. Freeman, July 1915**)

Faced with such testimony, the jury acquitted Emma B. Freeman of all charges, and Edwin withdrew from her life. The trial had increased Emma's notoriety, but she also achieved a measure of respect for her forthrightness. She had also achieved a public recognition for her artistic efforts during the two-year separation that tended to offset any infamy associated with her divorce.

In the weeks following their initial separation of July 1913, Edwin had left Eureka to follow a photographic career with the Northwestern Pacific Railroad Company. This action freed Emma to discard further pretension as to the conventions of their ill-fated marriage. She used this freedom to plunge into her work with a concentration exceeding any of her previous efforts. A public account of the Freeman Art Company's progress during the 1913-1915 period is provided by a subscribed entry in Irvine's *History of Humboldt County*, a 1915 listing of individuals and businesses:

*FREEMAN ART — the development of a large establishment out of the small business established in Eureka in 1906 is attributable to the capable efforts of Emma B. Freeman, the founder and present proprietor of the studio and a woman whose intense love of the beautiful and picturesque in nature led her in early childhood to follow the bright-plumaged birds to their hidden haunts in great trees; to study the flowers as they bloomed uncultivated and often unseen along the wayside; and to watch the changing cloud in the sky and every phase of scenery that allures the possessor of an artistic temperament. When she decided to develop her remarkable natural talent and to make drawing, painting, and photography her life work, she selected Humboldt County as the spot best adapted to her occupative duties. The results have proved that her selection was not amiss. It has been her privilege to tour practically every portion of northern California, taking with her a complete outfit of photographic necessities or a drawing and painting outfit. With these she has made pictures of the sun-kissed seashore, the isolated mountains, and the dense forests. A special atmosphere of romance seems to envelop these reproductions of picturesque spots and even a most casual glance at the large assortment of local pictures displayed in her studio proves her to be a true lover of nature and an expert in photography.*

**(History of Humboldt County, 1915)**

Confidently written, the above excerpt neatly sums up Emma's idealized self-concept. It also shows that Emma had at last found a practical means of self-expression. Until 1919, Emma utilized Eureka's Freeman Art Company not only as her source of economic security, but also as a focal-point for the art community in which she had emerged as an important spokesperson.

As an artist using a camera during this period, Emma had to contend with the strictures of the photographic establishment. One school of purists insisted that the artistic process stopped with the snapping of the shutter. This view held that the only creative acts available to the photographer were subject selection, composition, and simple exposure considerations. Another school, the photo-secessionists, blurred this distinction. It maintained an anything-goes attitude as long as the photograph was artistically conceived. Their aim was to break with conventional pictorialism, to explore fresh photographic subject matter, and to concentrate on the subtleties of light. Manipulation of both the negative and photographic print was a common feature of this group.

Emma was conscious of these various and strongly held opinions, through professional periodicals and the like, but she was physically isolated from the debate. In any event she was dead-set against capturing mere two-dimensional reality, for this immutable realism was the antithesis of Emma's artistic concepts. She aspired to reach an art form that combined drawing, painting and photography, one in which the artist's own hand was everywhere evident.

Emma's goal, judging by her own standards, was never fully reached. Even as her camera seized the outward essence of nature upon which it was focused, it failed to penetrate and satisfy her own vision of the mystery of nature as an inner experience. The elements of beauty and grace were represented, but too often she found the distant horizons of truth and poetry missing in the final result.

Judging by today's standards, it could be said that Emma did not attain her goal of a new mixed-media art for other reasons. Photography so dominated her visual expression that it relegated her painting and drawing to subordinate roles. She could not fully overcome the forthrightness inherent in photographic expression. Even the locale in which she worked provided another problem, its fleeting quality. As C. T. Wilson, painter of the California redwoods, commented at the time:

There are two distinct roads in photography — the utilitarian and the aesthetic; the goal of the one being a record of facts, and of the other an expression of beauty. They run parallel to each other, and many cross-paths connect them.

(Charles H. Caffin in
Photography as a fine art)

Nevertheless, her efforts were remarkable. Emma brought a unique vision to subject matter, for her approach to composition was heroic, her subject treatment allegorical, and her style painterly. Her surviving photographs clearly illustrate her training in the fine arts. Her groundbreaking efforts were made almost entirely on her own; in fact, her contemporaries in the region were purely traditional photographers. She alone enjoyed the reputation of "artist with the camera."

It was during this productive exploring period that Emma became more gregarious. Individuals to whom she had previously been attracted, but whom she had hesitated to enjoy in Ed's presence, now joined her. More than ever, the Freeman Art Company became a locus for impromptu gatherings.

Among her newer friends were women, sharing and expressing the feelings of rebellion she had experienced in the male-dominated society of Eureka. Also present were a small group of young people of mixed Indian and white parentage. Generally rejected by both communities, they were usually young adults born to Indian mothers. Fathers of these children were, for the most part, relatively skilled and self-sufficient white men who preferred to live in areas remote from the white community. Surprisingly, these individualists tended to regard education as an important goal for their children. In many cases, Emma's friends from this group were better schooled than either their Indian or white counterparts. Typically, the young people caught midway between two cultures had received their early education at a local United States Government Indian School, and many had attended Carlisle Indian School in Pennsylvania as well.

Carlisle Indian School was established in 1879 in an attempt to provide a means by which Native Americans might be assimilated into white society. Within its walls, strong efforts were made to end all tribal affiliations and religious practices; Indian ceremonies and organizations were banned. Instruction usually featured practical vocational training in such fields as farming, horticulture, dressmaking, cooking, laundering, and some twenty other trades. The Carlisle Indian School generally produced an attractive group of

Members of a shoemaking class at Carlisle Indian school.

young men and women — well equipped educationally to compete with whites, yet unable to participate effectively in the community at large because of deep-rooted racial prejudice. Rejection of the "half-breeds" by the Indian tribal community equalled that of white society. Although raised in emotional proximity to their Native American ancestry, they were denied access to the inner circles of Indian religion and leadership. The United States Government's educational policies stripped from them all vestiges of their Indian origin. The result was a total confusion of their cultural values.

In their association with Emma, these disenfranchised young adults found a person who publicly placed a high value on Indian craftsmanship and beauty. In addition, Emma reopened half-remembered events from their childhood and sought the suppressed details of their origin. She encouraged them to cherish the Indian culture of their mothers and to remember with pride their "noble Indian blood." Through her interest, the advantages of their link to two widely differing cultural backgrounds became preferable to the total abandonment of their Indian heritage in favor of white.

Emma regarded these tribal memories as central to her own involvement with nature. Linked in her own mind with life's mystical overtones, the American Indian symbolized a unity with the universal, the noble and divine wedding of man with the land. Her belief was perhaps characterized by Longfellow's heroic verse, *"Song of Hiawatha"*:

> *Should you ask me, whence these stories?*
> *Whence these legends and traditions,*
> *With the odors of the forest,*
> *With the dew and damp of meadows,*
> *With the curling smoke of wigwams,*
> *With the rushing of great rivers,*
> *With their frequent repetitions,*
> *And their wild reverberations,*
> *As of thunder in the mountains?*

It may be that Emma hoped these warm, romantic feelings would spring full-blown from hidden recesses in each person of Indian blood. Initially, a confused mixture of ideas and metaphors became evident as Emma was unable to reach the root sources of Indian culture. The misconceptions of white society as regards the Native American are legion and tragic (see appendix B).

Many times, on behalf of the Freeman Art Company, Emma had journeyed inland to the Yurok (Klamath River) and Hupa (Hoopa) tribal areas to purchase Indian baskets and other Native American crafts, both as merchandise and for display. Even this activity failed to bring her directly into contact with the reality of Indian awareness. The tribes in the Humboldt County region consisted of many branches and cultural levels. Even ethnologists and anthropologists of the era had considerable difficulty assigning meaningful tribal designations, because each family comprised a unique society. Emma's mixed bag of half-Indian, half-white friends thus represented a diversity of tribal affiliations. Indian groups which in earlier times may have been separated by a journey of several days were thrust into close proximity by the advent of modern transportation. Increased access only served to accentuate the confusion of tribal

Emma clad in the garb of her favorite subjects.

symbols and led, in a short time, to even greater cultural intermixing.

In the forefront of Emma's group of half-Indian friends was a personable young woman, Bertha M. Thompson. Also known as Princess Ah-tra-ah-saun, or Valley-of-the-Mountain, Bertha was the daughter of a full-blooded Klamath mother and a white timberman. Her early life was interestingly paraphrased in an interview by a San Francisco newsman:

*Princess Ah-tra-ah-saun left the forests and mountains of Northern California but a few years ago, coming out into a world of wonders that she knew only by hearsay. Until she was past 12 years of age she never saw a white woman. Practically the only white man she had known was her father, whose name she assumed when she left her native haunts. . . .* [Her father, Milton J.] *Thompson, a highly educated white man, gave his daughter the advantage of his knowledge, and unfolded to her eager curiosity strange tales of man-made machines that ran about on metal rails, of towering buildings made of steel, of the thousand and one utilities of modern civilization.*

*So great an effect did these stories make on Princess Ah-tra-ah-saun that when she was 18 years old, despite the kindness of her parents, she ran away from home and walked across the hills and valleys to Eureka. She had $11, which she had been years in the saving. With this she determined to secure an education . . . She at once entered school in Eureka, and there her father found her. But when he realized her power of mind and the intensity of her longing for knowledge, he had not the heart to bury her again in a place apart.*

**(San Francisco Chronicle, February 20, 1915)**

Bertha Thompson graduated from the Eureka public school in 1908, undertook nurse's training in a San Francisco hospital, and by 1913 was again in Eureka as a nurse for the Northern California Hospital Association. It was during this period that she first met Emma Freeman.

Emma was intrigued by Bertha's intimate knowledge of Indian life. With her awareness of nature's ways, Bertha Thompson made an ideal confidante for Emma. Until this time, the majority of Indians with whom she had come in contact were ragged, downtrodden individuals, or those fearful and suspicious of any attempt to photograph them. Although Bertha had spent recent years within white society, she had retained the native skills that she learned as a child along the Klamath River. Bertha was especially skilled at basketmaking and her work was prized for its craftsmanship.

The young half-Indian woman probably reminded Emma of her own childhood beginnings in Nebraska. Bertha had left her ancestral home at a formative age, as had Emma. Both had sacrificed to attain their goals. Both stood on the outskirts of their respective societies.

Bertha Thompson often visited the Freeman Art Company, and many of her handmade baskets and crafts were offered for sale there. It was during one of these visits that Emma first expressed to Bertha her wish to photograph her in Indian garments. Within a few days, Bertha and Emma traveled into the rugged region along the Klamath River and began taking photographs. These were not mere camera observations of tribal life, individuals, or villages. Rather, Emma placed Bertha in selected natural settings and carefully directed her poses, with a result that often bordered on the allegorical, in keeping with Emma's romantic interpretation of the Native American.

Emma B. Freeman was certainly not the first photographer to focus upon the American Indian. Photographic images of the continent's first citizens date from the mid-1800's. Many were frozen for eternity upon the mirrored surface of the daguerreotype, the first practical photographic process. Throughout photography's tenure in America, there have been thousands of historic images that reveal Indian lifestyles in the forestlands of the North and East, the vast plains of the Midwest and the arid plateaus of the Southwest. Nor was Emma the first to photograph the natives of the region of Northern California traversed by the Klamath and Trinity Rivers. In the two decades before the turn of the century, California photographer A. W. Ericson had gained a well-deserved reputation for his views of Indian townsites and people, posed within their natural or white-transitional environment. Particularly important among his efforts were images of the White Deerskin Dance, a major ceremonial of the area. By the time of Emma's trip to photograph the Klamath and Hoopa Indians, master-documentarian Edward S. Curtis was approaching the midpoint in his efforts to compile a remarkable photographic record of the North American Indian. Curtis' procedures perhaps exemplify the best possible approach to obtaining significant photographs of each native culture. He characteristically spent weeks living in close proximity to a tribe before attempting to employ his camera. On the whole, many photo-

(photograph opposite) Bertha M. Thompson (Princess Ah-Tra-Ah-Saun)

42

43

"Call of the Wild"

Northern California Series
By
Emma B. Freeman    Eureka Calif

44

graphers throughout the West had already recorded the rapidly disappearing phenomena of Indian life. The Indian photographs of Emma B. Freeman are not significant for their faithful approach in recording tribal ways. She did not wish to document the Indian per se, but aspired instead to express her inner concept of the Indian's noble heritage. In a pose at the edge of a rushing waterfall, titled, *"Indian Maid's Invocation,"* Bertha Thompson stands with her head thrown back and arms upstretched in supplication to Emma's vision of the Indian gods. Several variations in pose, photographed at the same site, include, *"Heart of Nature," "Land of Blue Waters,"* and *"Iaqua."* Her romantic images were well received by the townspeople of Northern California, but Emma was less satisfied.

Back from her Klamath expedition, Emma proceeded to paint a number of idealized wilderness backdrops for her studio. Working with her elaborately costumed models in this more controlled environment allowed her more freedom of lighting as well as background choice. *"Dawn,"* a bust portrait of an Indian maiden with a far distant gaze, is posed against a vividly painted morning sky. Even more elaborate backgrounds occur in such examples as *"Shasta Daisy"* and the *"Maid of Legends,"* photographs with painted fields of flowers, trees, and mountains. Emma also continued her exploration of natural settings. Some outdoor images, such as *"Ebb Tide,"* were taken along nearby coastal tide flats and beaches, while other examples show Emma's subject mirrored in a still woodland pool or crouched in a forest glade. Little of the subject's own personality is evident in these tableaux. Her models could easily have been replaced by mannequins.

It should be noted here that Emma did not create her ideas completely isolated from out-of-region influences. Many periodicals of the era regularly featured the work of other Western artists. Literary journals of the period discussed the universe in terms of primeval forces: Fire, Earth, Water, Life, Love, and Death — and led to art titled *"Man receiving instruction in Nature's laws."* Indian life was a most popular subject. *"What an Indian Thinks"* might be a typical title for a symbolistic painting of the Native American. It is most likely that Emma personally knew Grace Hudson and her fine paintings of Pomo Indian children. Hudson worked in the Ukiah, California area, which was on the overland road midway between Eureka and San Francisco. The efforts of photographers Karl Moon, Edward M. Langley and others to pictorialize the Indians of the

(photograph opposite) "Call of the Wild" one of a group of images taken in selected natural sites in the Klamath River region of Northern California. "Oh, for an hour away from care in this wilderness of wooded joy, where quiet and peace comes wafting down from God's great paradise."

45

Southwest were familiar to Emma. She also maintained contact with her friends in San Francisco and often visited the city itself.

Although Emma photographed a number of different men and women, Bertha Thompson remained one of her favorite models, and was destined to play an important role in other events that were soon to follow.

Bertha's mother, Lucy Thompson, was a full-blooded member of the Yurok tribal family which lived along the Klamath River. Born in 1853, in the community of Pecwan, her early relationship with white men had made her the subject of a complex family prejudice. The Indian community shunned her, and she had lived in the grey area between two cultures. Marriage to Bertha's father, a white man named Milton J. Thompson, proved to be a happy turning point in her life. Thompson, a successful timberman, was sensitive to Lucy's Indian heritage, and helped her maintain a fine collection of tribal garments and artifacts. Many of the Indian costumes that appear in Emma's images were borrowed from this legacy. Lucy, with the help of her husband and daughter, prepared a manuscript in the last years of her life on the history and customs of her Klamath River ancestors. Written most thoughtfully, *To the American Indian"* was published in 1916 and revealed Lucy's — and Bertha's — heritage:

Lucy Thompson, Yurok author of *To the American Indian,* **1916.**

*I am a pure full-blooded Klamath River woman. In our tongue, we call this great river by the name Health-kick-werroy, and I wore the tattoos on my chin that has been the custom for our women for many generations. I was born at Pecwan village, and of highest birth of what we term under the highest laws of marriage. I am known by my people as a talth. My maiden name was Che-na-wah Weitch-ah-wah, Che-na-wah being my given name. My father being also a talth, took me at a very early age and began training me in all the mysteries and laws of my people. It took me years to learn and the ordeal was a hard one . . . I can understand every word, every nod and gesture made in our language. Therefore I feel that I am in a better position than any other person to tell the true facts of the religion and the meaning of the many things that we used to commemorate the events of the past . . .*

**(To the American Indian, 1916)**

Her book was published by a little-known print shop and never achieved wide circulation, yet it remains a remarkable document, rich in the detail of tribal lore. Even though it was narrated in

(photograph opposite) Part of a series of experiments that Emma undertook in her studio. Strong directional lighting and painterly compositions are a typical mark of her work.

47

S. Fred Chamley

English, her second language, Lucy's clarity of meaning was excellent. Through her daughter, Lucy undoubtedly influenced Emma's understanding of local Indian culture.

Another important member of Emma's growing circle of friends was S. F. (Fred) Chamley, who had arrived in Eureka early in 1914 from Los Angeles. Chamley's father had been a minister, and he wanted Fred to join his older brother in training for the pulpit. Striving to avoid family conflict, but determined to avoid a clerical life, 17-year old Chamley set out to earn his own way. Part Cherokee Indian, tall and attractive, Fred discovered the Freeman Art Company, where Emma offered him employment in the shop doing odd jobs.

Because Fred was an interested and willing worker, he soon participated in all aspects of the store. In time, he felt confident enough to offer Emma his suggestions on measures to improve her camera technique and efficiency. This exasperated and distracted Emma, who suggested that he try his own hand at the camera and darkroom. To her surprised satisfaction, the results of his amateur experimentation seemed promising, and young Chamley soon proved an invaluable assistant.

Throughout Fred's interaction with Emma, he was an ideal associate in many ways. Although he was clever and helpful, he did not challenge Emma's authority to run things in her way, even though he commonly questioned ideas and procedures. They worked in a prideful intimacy that was nurtured by the everyday tasks they shared. For Emma, Chamley was both a faithful employee and a respected co-worker. Long days at the store were the rule:

*Commencing the day at 7 a. m., they had worked straight through with only small breaks for lunch and supper . . . it was well after 10 p. m. when Emma suggested, "Fred, why don't you quit early tonight and get started again early in the morning?"*

**(Interview, Bertha Stevens Chamley, Spring 1976)**

Chamley, who had found in photography a calling that was to extend beyond Emma's tutelage, remained with the Freeman Art Company even after she sold the shop. He was a practical man who filled Emma's need for diligence and efficiency. More importantly, his participation allowed Emma additional time to develop contacts with her Native American friends.

The Freeman Art Company, with Emma firmly in charge, became the respected custodian of Indian culture for a sizeable portion of Northern California. Indian crafts demonstrations, with displays of related handcrafts, were often held. The *Humboldt Standard* mentioned that, on such occasions, the store would be *"decorated inside very artistically with small trees and shrubbery, the scent of which gives the visitor the call of the outdoors upon entering the studio."* The same newspaper was enthused to comment on Emma's Indian portraits:

*An artist has come out of the hills and brought with her lasting pictures of the fast fading memories of yesterday — pictures of Indians, their home life, environments, rare spots of beauty, pictures of hills, streams, waterfalls, mountains and rocks. The artist is Emma B. Freeman . . . To obtain these art gems, Mrs. Freeman gained the friendship of an Indian princess, then journeyed with her into the hills, traveling over the rough trails into the heart of the great silent spots of the mountains and forests. Her camera and colors tell the story . . . The [art] subjects are in two splendidly large sizes and in sepia, grey and colors, with these titles: Ancient Law, Allegiance, Ah-tra-ah-saun (meaning Valley of the Mountain), Bartered Bride, Call of the Blood, Call of the Wild, Dawn, Daughter of the Klamath, Enchantress, Eureka, Ebbtide, Five Generations, Golden West, Mizpah, Goddess of Feast, Heart of Nature, In the Land of the Gods, Iaqua (meaning salutation), Klamath Tango, Land of the Setting Sun, Little Provider, Lost Trail, Land of Blue Waters, Maid of Legends, Out of the Past, Red Arrow, Red Man's Dream . . .*

**(Humboldt Standard, January 27, 1917)**

*The collection is called the Northern California series, and portrays many beautiful Indian types from the Hupa and Klamath reservations . . . portraying as they do the dawn of a new race, and having all the mystery, beauty and grace about which romance is woven.*

**(Humboldt Standard, February 4, 1915)**

*Sunset* magazine also commented on Emma's accomplishments: *"When first she gained confidence in the Art of Photography, it was a personal pleasure* [for Emma] *to take pictures of her Indian friends and to show them their 'Shadows!' . . ."* In an article entitled, *"With Nature's Children,"* Emma spoke about her feelings:

49

*. . . the average Indian is extremely opposed to facing the camera. This is because of a tribal tradition which forbids handling the dead or preserving anything ever owned or worn by the departed; only their memory is left and that an unspoken thought . . .*

*As a basis of legend and literature for future generations I have endeavored to preserve in picture what scholars and literature have preserved in story, viz., the very best in the life history of the American Indian.*

**(Pacific Outdoors, October 1917)**

As Emma achieved recognition for her efforts at Indian portraiture, she was able to extend her reach into the full-blooded Indian community for new subjects. Frank Robert Spott was a particularly important new acquaintance. He possessed first-hand knowledge of tribal matters and may have been among the first to recognize the need for a permanent photographic record of tribal ways. Robert Spott was thoroughly grounded in the history and lore, law and religion, and the medicine and ceremonies of his race. With an intuitive awareness, he perceived the end of traditional tribal life and, to ensure its record, was prepared to admit Emma into his confidence. Among the photographs of Spott by Freeman are valuable views which record the use of redwood dugout canoes on the Klamath River. Spott inevitably appeared in Emma's photos correctly attired in selected tribal garments. In one pictorial series, he garbed himself in a succession of tribal regalia, intended for use in his culture's ceremonials. These images are vaguely reminiscent of fashion photographs. Spott posed on a riverbank, displaying each garment, headdress, and accessory that had meaning for a particular tribal event. Most of these costumes were spectacular in appearance and were even more striking when worn properly. Many examples from this series were used to illustrate an article published in the April, 1917 *Overland Monthly*, entitled, *"Ah-Pura-Way, the Dance of the White Deerskin and Other Indian Worship Dances."* The accompanying article, written by Edna Hildebrand Putnam, has heavy evangelical overtones, and is rampant with condescension. Even so, it contained several accurate quotations from Robert Spott concerning the ceremonials:

*It is whenever there being so many kinds of sickness upon the earth. The earth is dried — no green grass and the wild flowers and all the birds are flying away; and so all the animals going away too. No*

Robert Spott in the ceremonial garb of the White Deerskin Dance.

50

*berries, no acorns, no fish upon the river. Then a medicine man go up in the high mountain and prayed to the heavens and to the stars and to the sun with his power that sickness will be going away and have a better world: the earth will be covered with green grass and wild flowers and plenty of fish in the river — also berries and all animals and birds will come back to earth again.*

*. . . This dance always have whenever the people hear a sickness coming on a far away . . . A medicine man sit beside the fire and has a long pipe and smoke Indian tobacco and not drink water and eat once day. Then he pray to heaven, and before he sit down he took*

Emma B. Freeman Native American tableau set on the banks of the Klamath River, circa 1915.

51

*Indian tobacco and put a little on his hand. Then he blow to north and south with his power that sickness will not reach here, and again he blow to the east and the west. Then he sit down ... Then the dance beginning do dance around him and people looking on are all feeling very sadness.*

(Overland Monthly, April 1917)

Spott was a leader in moving his people towards co-existence with the white man. During World War I, he served with distinction in the armed forces as a personal scout for General John Pershing. At war's end, Spott returned to his home to continue his efforts on behalf of his people.

If Robert Spott and Bertha Thompson had been both symbols and confidants to Emma in the preparation of her Indian photographs, it required the presence of another Bertha to provide insights into the portions of Emma's personality that were consistently camouflaged by her public image as an artist. Into her life now came Bertha Stevens, who was born at the Klamath River settlement of Orleans to an Indian mother and a white father employed as a miner. In childhood she attended Carlisle Indian School for five years, majoring in Home Economics. Upon her return from Pennsylvania, she was reunited with Grace Wayman, her favorite, older half-sister. The two girls shared their plans and ambitions for the future, including their prospects for marriage.

The "Gibson Man" had evolved, by 1914, into one of the popular male stereotypes. Bertha and her sister frequently idealized the type of individual that would most suit them as husbands. One day, while passing the Freeman Art Company, Bertha caught a glimpse of Fred Chamley. She later reported to her sister that she had *"just seen her Gibson Man."* Applying at the store for work, she was hired by Emma Freeman to retouch photographs and to aid in their hand-coloring.

Throughout this time, Emma lived on the mezzanine floor of the store. Although this provided her with relatively little space, it included a cooking area, sitting room, and screened bedroom. Bertha soon shared this crowded apartment with Emma, doing much of the cooking for her employer, Fred and their visitors.

Emma quickly became fast friends with the lighthearted girl, sharing confidences and intimacies in a sisterly way. Over sixty years later, Bertha reminisced about their friendship:

*She was pleasant and full of fun . . . and had a fine capacity for putting people at ease. Men especially liked Emma. Even though the store demanded a great deal of attention, we gossiped a lot . . . and enjoyed our friends. Minnie [Mary Steinhauer], another local artist often visited the shop and we all would have lunch together and visit a lot . . . sometimes all day . . . We had great fun. Emma dressed in an eccentric manner, sometimes with boots and a man's hat with rattlesnake skin around its crown. I made her a tailored suit which she was very happy [with] . . . and wore a lot. Emma was playful and sisterly. She liked me to do her hair . . . style it and so on.*

*Emma had good business sense, her gallery had a display of photos to prompt the visitor's interest . . . lots of paintings and Indian baskets and crafts, everywhere. The idea of "appointments" was not much and often a visitor would select an idea from the display and pose for Emma on the spot.*

*She often physically touched people in posing them, wanting them just so . . . and her posing had an "artificial" appearance . . .*

*She lighted her subjects heavily from one side giving them a strong shadow on one side of their face . . . Fred complained that it was hard to print in the darkroom . . . and you couldn't see things in the shadow . . .*

*She liked to experiment and had very odd . . . nocturnal work habits, often working all night, or getting up at 3 am.*

*Emma and Fred did not agree about painting style and technique . . . she was also somewhat careless in her darkroom habits [and] . . . left things laying about.*

*Emma sold many paintings . . . not so many of her own, but she handled well known artists like Mrs. Wright who specialized in redwood paintings.*

**(Interview, Bertha Stevens Chamley, Spring 1976)**

Bertha Stevens, Emma's close friend and confidante.

The relationship between these two young women grew steadily closer. On one occasion, when Bertha had fallen ill with a very high fever, Emma insisted on taking her to the nearby Vance Hotel for a "hot bath and broth." Emma was nearly forced to carry the weakened Bertha to the hotel. She stayed with her for hours until the fever lessened. On another occasion, Bertha related:

*Emma was not a very good [automobile] driver and one time when we were going to the north to visit, we came to a long hill near Trinidad . . . Emma was going too fast down the hill and the car went back and forth until it ran off the road and went over on its side. We were not hurt but there was no one to help us at that time, so we waited . . . after a while we got out Emma's camera and went away from the road and, had great fun taking pictures of each other . . . sometimes without our clothes.*

(Interview, Bertha Stevens Chamley, Spring 1976)

Of half Indian origin herself, Bertha was generally pleased with Emma's Indian portraits, except those images that depicted women performing men's duties. Among those photographs which Bertha felt were unsatisfactory is a series in which a woman is depicted with a warrior's bow and arrows. In most of the earlier photos, Emma's Indian subjects were not always authentically clothed. Bertha also objected to the use of a prop Navajo blanket and the inclusion of a Shasta basket hat that was not traditional local costume.

In March 1917, Bertha Stevens married her "Gibson Man," Fred Chamley. The new Mrs. Chamley was 24, her groom 21. Although she did not continue to work after her marriage, Bertha often visited the store as Emma's close friend and continuing confidante.

While Bertha Thompson, Robert Spott and Bertha Chamley were the most frequent figures in Emma's Indian photographs, a number of other individuals posed for the Indian series. These included Jessie Cleveland, Hazel Ferris, Vivian Chase, Ina Bussell, Iva Hickcock, and Grace Wayman. With the exception of Robert Spott, and Ed Pearch, most of the names of the males who posed for Emma have been forgotten. On at least one occasion, Emma used a blond European model, darkening his hair, spreading theatrical makeup on his face, selecting an Indian wardrobe, and photographing the swarthy Indian brave.

Once firmly established, Emma commonly combined her painting and drawing techniques with her skill at photography. In addition to preparing artistically-conceived, hand-painted backdrops to serve as environments for her studio portraits, she supervised the hand-coloring of black and white photographic images. Typically, color was applied to these photographs with brushed-on transparent paints, but examples of heavy opaque oils also exist. In the latter case, the photograph itself served merely as a basis for design, and the finished work most nearly resembled a painting.

Emma's brush and pencil work is distinguishable from that of the other colorists of the Freeman Art Company. In her hands, the

Bertha Stevens and Emma at the site of the automobile runaway.

application of color or pencil was an additional artistic element. This served to make coloring of the photographs an extension of the artist's vision rather than a simple attempt at realism. One example was her common treatment of head-and-shoulder portraits. A vignetted photographic portrait often tended to appear isolated against its light background, with the image giving the illusion of "floating" in its frame. To combat this tendency, Emma used a heavy pencil to add a series of lines at the base of the portrait. These lines were coupled with Emma's signature and formed a pedestal upon which the portrait could be anchored. *Studio Light*, official organ of the Eastman Kodak Company, commented on her use of this device:

*"In most cases these* [Emma's portraits] *are clean vignetted prints with just enough pencil work to lend a touch of individuality and relieve the portrait of any heavyness* [sic]*."*

**(Studio Light, June 1915)**

55

"On the Great Devide"

Northern California Series
By
Emma B. Freeman
Eureka Cal.

In some instances Emma used pastels to add vistas or the suggestion of figures to the background of her photographic images. One of her Indian series, called *"On the Great Divide,"* features, for example, a distant horizon with horse-borne Indians traveling into the distance in single file. In this case, both the horizon and the horsemen had been created through Emma's use of pastels.

In time, a full set of Emma's Indian studies numbered approximately 200 images and was known as the Northern California Series. The prints themselves, usually 6½ x 8½ inches in size, were contact-printed from heavy, cumbersome, glass-plate negatives that were subject to breakage when carelessly handled. Because the camera lens that she used was designed primarily for portraits, the photos were somewhat soft-focused and generally unsharp. In some instances, Emma deliberately increased this unsharpness during exposure by using large lens openings, or, in the darkroom, by spacing the glass-plate negative from the printing paper during the print-making process. Finished photographs were prepared on oversize paper in which the image was frequently surrounded with one or more soft-toned grey or brown bands. In some sets, an Indian design was incorporated as a decorative touch along the margin of the print. The image color often varied widely, extending from a warm, greyish-brown to a spectacular deep russet. Emma nearly always signed her work, usually in pencil, as *"Emma B. Freeman,"* or occasionally *"E. B. Freeman."*

The Northern California Series was often sold in sets, but varied both in the quantity and selection of included images. A number of complete sets were shipped abroad to such countries as France, Canada, and Japan. There also existed a smaller set of vignetted Indian portraits, known appropriately as the Indian Head Series. Enlargements as big as 16 x 20 inches were made from the more popular images. These were suitable for framing and became popular parlor pieces. The Freeman Art Store regularly displayed a large selection of Emma's Indian portraits on its gallery walls.

For several years, extensive plans had been underway for the San Francisco Panama-Pacific International Exposition. Over 40 states and nearly as many foreign countries had prepared exhibits intended to provide a glimpse of the very best in technology and cultural accomplishment to the expected throngs of visitors. The fair opened on February 20, 1915, and was a masterpiece of planning and design. The grounds of the Exposition itself covered an area along the shore

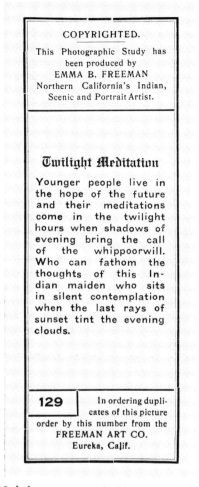

COPYRIGHTED.

This Photographic Study has been produced by
EMMA B. FREEMAN
Northern California's Indian, Scenic and Portrait Artist.

**Twilight Meditation**

Younger people live in the hope of the future and their meditations come in the twilight hours when shadows of evening bring the call of the whippoorwill. Who can fathom the thoughts of this Indian maiden who sits in silent contemplation when the last rays of sunset tint the evening clouds.

**129**  In ordering duplicates of this picture order by this number from the FREEMAN ART CO. Eureka, Calif.

Labels were attached to the folio mount of each photograph of the Northern California Series. Other examples of Emma Freeman's prose also appear in our portfolio as captions.

(photograph opposite) "On the Great Divide" illustrates the use of pastels to create ethereal riders in the background. Emma often pre-painted backgrounds or painted and drew directly on the finished print to provide natural or episodic information for her audience.

of San Francisco Bay one-half mile wide by two and one-half miles long.

Transportation facilities to the site carried 50,000 visitors per hour, and ample hotel facilities were guaranteed for any number of travelers. The Panama-Pacific International Exposition was billed as the only world exposition where climatic conditions enabled the outdoor display of mural paintings on canvas. Within the galleries of the fine arts, hundreds of the world's most acclaimed artists were to participate. An extensive fine arts pavilion had been constructed to house the art displays. However, not all of the art was located in this structure. Only a few yards down the street, a subsidiary display was to draw a disproportionate amount of comment from the fairgoers.

Although the Humboldt County region in which Emma worked was a late-comer in terms of its preliminary planning, it had prepared an extensive exhibit for display at the exposition. Within a 43 x 96 foot booth located in the California Building, it featured a diversified display of forestry, dairying and other agriculture. The most prominent feature of the exhibit was a huge structure made of a single, 20-foot-diameter redwood stump. Inside was a miniature art gallery that included 31 Emma B. Freeman Indian portraits, as well as several large scenic paintings by Eureka's artists.

Several events focused recognition on Emma's display at the Exposition. In Eureka, over 1,000 visitors toured the Freeman Art Company to see a full set of her Indian portraits from which the selected group would be drawn. Then, accompanied by Klamath Princess Ah-tra-ah-saun in full Indian regalia, Emma traveled with her exhibit to San Francisco. On her arrival, she set up a popular display in a downtown hotel several days prior to the fair's start, exhibiting one set of her Northern California Series. She also contacted local newspapers to make them aware of her role in the upcoming show. Thus, on the opening day of the Panama-Pacific International Exposition, the prestigious *San Francisco Chronicle* featured in its lead story:

*ROYAL INDIAN MAID IN TODAY'S PARADE*
*WILL LEAD NATIVE DAUGHTERS COLUMN*
*HONOR FOR PRINCESS AH-TRA-AH-SAUN.*

The extensive and laudatory account also featured several front page photographs:

Fair Commissioner W. S. Clark today selected and purchased 31 of Mrs. Emma B. Freeman's Indian portraits to be placed in the Humboldt exhibit at the Panama-Pacific Exposition. Many of the portraits have been beautifully hand colored by Mrs. Freeman . . .

(Humboldt Standard, February 10, 1915)

*. . . from life, photographed by Mrs. Emma B. Freeman whose picture [also] appears . . . The princess and the pictures will be part of Humboldt County's Indian Exhibit at the exposition.*

(San Francisco Chronicle, February 20, 1915)

Emma's continuing ability to have her likeness published in newspapers and magazines was phenomenal. In an elaborate special edition, for example, the *Humboldt Times* published photographs of all the mayors, city councilmen, clergymen, bankers, judges, and other prominent citizens from Humboldt County. Amid the public figures was Emma B. Freeman's portrait, reproduced at least four times larger than any other in the issue. In a similar vein, when Emma had photographed the famous orator, William Jennings Bryan, at her Eureka studio, the *Humboldt Standard* ran a sizeable account of the event. Accompanying the story, where one might expect the display of Bryan's image, was the now much-reproduced portrait of Emma.

Public reaction to Emma Freeman's participation at the Panama-Pacific International Exposition was consistently laudatory. Long lines of visitors thronged the Humboldt County exhibit, and Emma's photographs were widely discussed.

She received extensive inquiries about her Indian portraits, including many requests to purchase copies. The *Humboldt Times* editorialized this growing professional esteem in an article titled, *"Our Advance in Art"*:

*. . . the camera has revolutionized the popular conception of art . . . Our sunsets on the broad Pacific would delight the soul of a Turner. The rocky headlands and sandy stretches of beaches, with their [ship] wrecks and picturesque fisher folks would inspire a Moran . . . it may [therefore] surprise many of our own people to know that through the efforts of the Freeman Art Company of this city over five thousand Indian subjects alone have been produced, in addition to many thousands more of attractive and beautiful Humboldt County scenes . . .*

(Humboldt Times, December 6, 1915)

In the rival *Humboldt Standard*, the years immediately following the Panama-Pacific International Exposition were summarized with these observations:

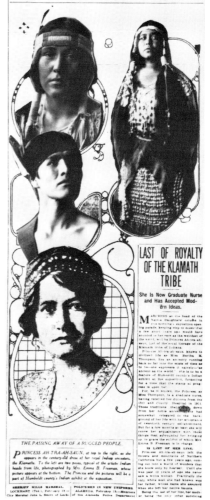

Royal Indian Maid in Today's Parade
Will Lead Native Daughters' Column
Honor for Princess Ah-Tra-Ah-Saun

LAST OF ROYALTY
OF THE KLAMATH
TRIBE

She Is Now Graduate Nurse
and Has Accepted Modern Ideas.

THE PASSING AWAY OF A RUGGED PEOPLE.

PRINCESS AH-TRA-AH-SAUN, at top to the right, as she appears in the century-old dress of her royal Indian ancestors, the Klamaths. To the left are two poses, typical of the artistic Indian heads from life, photographed by Mrs. Emma B. Freeman, whose picture appears at the bottom. The Princess and the pictures will be a part of Humboldt county's Indian exhibit at the exposition.

*Clippings from leading newspapers and magazines including Leslie's, The Illustrated Review, Studio Light, Sunset, Camera Craft, Overland Monthly, Pacific Outdoors, the S. F. Chronicle, the S. F. Examiner, and dozens of others as well known and with national circulations, testify to her international prominence . . . Letters from England, France, Italy, Russia, South America and Japan, commenting favorably on her work and including orders for her studies . . . Figured on a basis of space values, the publicity obtained by Mrs. Freeman in the great national dailies and magazines runs into the hundreds of thousands of dollars.*

**(Humboldt Standard, June 4, 1918)**

In order to accommodate her rapidly-expanding business, Emma added a new display location in downtown Eureka. Known as the "Gift Shop", this facility was destined, in time, to replace the previous quarters and to become a permanent home for the Freeman Art Company. The upper floors of the new store included a modern studio. Newspaper advertisements described the shop: *"The art rooms are upstairs, including a large operating room, parlor, hall used for display of Indian and artistic photos, dressing rooms, finishing room, two printing rooms, an enlarging room, and a developing room."*

The gift and sales area was operated by Harvey B. Burnett. Burnett, previously employed as a salesman by the Humboldt Timber and Land Company, joined the Freeman Art Company in 1914-15. Beginning on a part-time basis, he later became sales manager of the store.

Born in California of English parentage, Burnett spoke without an accent, but with the verbal overtones of a "proper" Englishman. He was considered well-educated by his customers and had succeeded in nurturing a reputation as an art expert. Besides improving the attractiveness of the store through clever displays, Burnett added the sophisticated atmosphere usually found in more metropolitan areas. On the other hand, he was frequently described as overly smooth, and had a reputation as a quick man with money. He invariably appeared well-dressed, but surrounding his attire was the story that he *"purchased several dozen suits at a local bargain sale and had his tailor rework them so that they appeared to be handmade."* Despite these questionable qualities, he was a good salesman and had a certain following in the community for his ability to speak

(photograph opposite) A page from the *Illustrated Review* of March 1918 featuring Emma's portraits.

60

# Indian Girls of Symmetry and Grace

**An Indian Madonna**

A MARVELOUS face that grows more beautiful with time. Troubles and dissensions come to her and quietly and tenderly she adjusts the wrongs among her people.

**Call of the Blood**

IT has been rightly declared that "an Indian never forgets." This girl clothed in the raiment of her people is watching through a lighted window an enemy of her tribe.

**"Ah Tra ah Sann"**

MEANING "Valley of the Mountain." This little Indian maiden was selected to lead the procession at the opening of the great San Francisco Exposition.

**Out of the Past**

HER heritage is marvelous beauty and strength and the rich hair and olive skin of the blended blood. It is a portrait that stirs the mind.

© Emma B. Freeman, Eureka, Cal.

—15—

61

Emma in her second-floor studio at the Gift Shop location. Note the stylized backdrops and the nude study displayed in her right hand.

substantively about art. Burnett continued as an important member of the Freeman Art Company throughout Emma's tenure in the business. With Burnett as salesman and Fred Chamley taking over most of the darkroom work, Emma's goal of freeing herself from the company's daily management was achieved.

It was an indication of Emma Freeman's newly-won reputation that few people thought it improper when she chose to produce a number of nude studies in her new studio. Although these photographs have been lost, the content of two was remembered. In one, a lithe young woman reclined near a small waterfall in a woodland setting; the other was a studio pose of a woman with a harp. Both were highly romantic studies, consistent with the other works of art on display in Emma's storefront. The public accepted these nudes without protest, as an extension of Emma's interest in art. The efforts of another local photographer of the period, however, were rewarded more harshly. He received a year in prison for his attempt at photographic nudes.

Emma had clearly demonstrated her serious intent in the production of artistic statements. Besides attracting favorable national recognition to her region and self, she finally attained the measure of local recognition that she had once sought so desperately. The Freeman Art Company had become a successful business. Her circle of friends and admirers was at its peak. Then, into this idyllic setting, world events intervened which quickly added a new dimension to her life.

On the night of December 14, 1916, a United States submarine vessel ran aground on a sandbar adjacent to Humboldt Bay. One of a small fleet of submersibles, the *H-3* was in the company of its supply ship, the Monitor *Cheyenne*, when it became lost in heavy fog. The vessel was photographed in its distress by many photographers, including Emma B. Freeman. The publicity greatly embarrassed the United States Navy. At first, the Navy had thought to tow the little vessel from its entrapment, but the heavy seas had rendered its power supply inoperable. A local salvage company offered to extricate the 360-ton *H-3* from its sandbar prison for $18,000. The Navy instead sent two seagoing tugs up from San Francisco and made several unsuccessful attempts to dislodge the submarine. Frustrated, the Navy then decided that the *H-3* could be refloated with the help of the heavy cruiser *Milwaukee,* a prime warship valued at over seven million dollars.

For several days, the *Milwaukee* maneuvered perilously near the beach and its forlorn submarine. At best, it would be a difficult salvage. With the reputation of the Navy at stake, however, the cruiser succeeded in attaching a tow line to the *H-3*. As the warship strained, it appeared for a few moments that the effort would succeed. Then, strong currents and the drag of the tow, combined with a heavy fog that made signalling difficult, pulled the cruiser into the ever treacherous surf. Soon the *Milwaukee* was hopelessly trapped.

Emma B. Freeman photographed every aspect of the disaster, including the subsequent rescue by breeches-buoy of the cruiser's crew. Bypassing the local newspapers, she immediately rushed her

# San Francisco Chronicle

1865

SAN FRANCISCO, CAL., MONDAY, JANUARY 15, 1917

**UKEE IS
N SAND
ISTING**

## First Pictures of Stranded Cruiser Milwaukee, With Work of Rescuing Her Crew in Progress

The Milwaukee as she lies after piling up on the beach near the entrance to Eureka harbor Saturday. This remarkable photograph was taken while Jack Deeke, the first man to be rescued from the unfortunate warship, was being brought ashore in a breeches buoy. Others were rescued by the same means, while still others were taken off in boats. The Milwaukee now lies a few yards up the beach from where she struck, with a list of 40 degrees to seaward. An expert engineer made a survey of the vessel yesterday and gave it as his opinion that there is no hope of saving her. (Photo by Freeman Art Company.)

Wonderful D
Space in U
M. H.

CERAMICS

Vases Mode
Masters Lu
to Go

While some of the crew of the stranded vessel were brought ashore in the breeches buoy, others were rescued in boats which plowed their way through the surf to the ship and back again. The photograph shows the boat commanded by N. E. Darling on its fifth trip from the Milwaukee during the work of rescue.

### Cruiser Cannot Be Floated, Says Expert Engineer

EUREKA, January 14.—The cruiser Milwaukee cannot be floated, it was announced here today by J. D. Fraser, expert mechanical engineer, who at the solicitation of Lieutenant W. J. Newton, in command, today made a complete survey of the stranded cruiser.

## SAN FRANCISCO PIONEER, 90, IS TAKEN BY DEATH

Garrett John Byrne, First Bridegroom of Old St. Mary's, Passes

## Passengers in Panic, Boats Lowered, When Ships Collide

Steamer Umatilla Rams Schooner Daisy Putnam at San

## MUDHEN WINS DEFENSE FROM NATURE EXPERT

Coot, or Los Angeles Mallard, Not Hell-Diver, Says Sergeant Mc-

Mines De
Ship; C

photographs to San Francisco, where they formed the basis of a front-page, pictorial article in the *San Francisco Chronicle*.

The two photographs chosen by the *Chronicle* excellently captured the tense drama of this marine disaster. In all, 449 men and officers were rescued from the *Milwaukee*. Publicity was widespread, and Emma's reputation continued to soar as she won praise from a nation accustomed to male-dominated photojournalism.

Rear Admiral W. B. Caperton, Commander of the Pacific Fleet, personally appeared at the site of the disaster to inspect salvage procedures. Emma was subsequently appointed as the official photographer by the Navy Department in matters concerning the stranding of the *Milwaukee*. The *San Francisco Chronicle* recorded the event in an article titled *"U. S. REWARDS PLUCKY WOMAN PHOTOGRAPHER"*:

*Every day since the Milwaukee went ashore, Mrs. Freeman has been on the job with her camera. She has taken more than 200 photographs of the wrecked vessel, most of them under the most trying conditions of fog and wind and weather. From the surf-beaten beach, from rowboats and from ships outside she has photographed the Milwaukee from every angle . . .*

(San Francisco Chronicle, January 31, 1917)

She was also successful in her attempts to persuade Rear Admiral Caperton to pose for her camera, although the Admiral was strongly prejudiced against being photographed and had not posed for a picture since 1881. In the ensuing weeks, passersby at the Freeman Art Company were treated to a large display, including the American flag, and photographs of the *H-3, Milwaukee*, Admiral Caperton, and his staff.

In her capacity as "Official Government Photographer," Emma continued to make headlines *"WOMAN INVADES WATERY HULL OF MILWAUKEE"*:

*Rats in the hold of the water-logged cruiser Milwaukee, that lies stranded on the Samoa beach, were given a surprise yesterday when Mrs. Emma B. Freeman . . . invaded their haunts in the watery darkenss.*

*The feat was a daring one for a woman, the list of the vessel, the swish-swash of the waters in the inky blackness and the slippery footholds making it a difficult performance for a man.*

### THE H-3

Oh, little H-3
Why in H — did you go
On the beach at Samoa,
Is what I'd like to know.

Do you see what you've done,
By your antics so queer:
In spite of all things,
There's a naval base here.

And the Cheyenne, your mother,
What a temper she's in:
Brought on by her child's
Disobedience and sin.

And the cruiser Milwaukee,
With her crew once so gay,
Is a broken old hulk,
tossed by waves in their play.

And the sailors in blue,
What they've said about you;
Would not bear the printing,
Tho' tis every word true.

You may glide through water,
Like a fair ocean queen;
But the beach is no place,
For a gay submarine.

Mabel S. Heymann
(Humboldt Times, 28, January 1917)

*The courageous photographer, with ropes secured around her to keep her from slipping into the water, managed to descend into the vessel and by creeping about on slippery decks over which the water splashed with every tilt of the vessel, managed to get the views sought.*

**(San Francisco Bulletin, February 19, 1917)**

Always inclined to an irregular work schedule, Emma worked without reference to the clock throughout this busy time. After each new foray to the wreck, the Freeman Art Company windows featured the latest views of the *Milwaukee's* distress. Portrait and other studio traffic increased proportionately with her fame. It seemed for a time that Emma had found herself a niche in photojournalism as well as art, but the rumblings in Europe were echoing throughout Northern California with a clamor louder than the sound of the waves crashing against the hull of the wrecked *Milwaukee.*

Long the focus of news in Europe, World War I was now actively involving the United States. Gone were glib references to "kicking the Hun back over the Rhine." America was preparing to join the battle with her own sons' blood. As an increasing sense of national outrage at reported German atrocities grew in the hearts of Americans, newspaper editorials touted themes of "preparedness" and encouraged their readers to "fight to the end."

Throughout the war, Emma displayed a public profile that was surprisingly patriotic. Her interest seemed improbable, for she had never taken an active interest in social or political causes. As the prospect of the war grew nearer, she undertook a number of supportive pledges to various service organizations, as the following letter, written to the editor of the *Humboldt Times*, exemplifies:

*Editor,*
*I desire, through you, to subscribe $1 monthly for the duration of the war, to the fund of the Eureka branch of the American Legion of California. Check for current month enclosed herewith.*

**(Humboldt Times, April 13, 1917)**

It was also widely reported that Emma B. Freeman had volunteered "to photograph at the front." Such pledges were designed, in part, to publicly show her posture of patriotism. It was wise to proclaim strong patriotic feelings through such deeds, for the

## THE KILLING COSTUME

The ladies try to catch the eye
   With hats and dresses new,
The college lad is just as bad,
   And airs his fashions, too.
But after all, in spring or fall,
   This truth remaineth still,
The soldier boy's the only guy
   That's all dressed up to kill.

— Judge.
(Humboldt Times, March 1, 1916)

66

slightest evidence of non-involvement in the war effort was frequently interpreted as cowardice or treason.

Throughout her forays into photojournalism and patriotic fervor, Emma Freeman still found time to continue her series of Indian photographs. Unlike her earlier efforts, however, she now turned her camera on the aged remnants of the tribal communities. Record-like, most of these views were taken on the Indian reservations at Hoopa and Klamath. Typical photographs of this time include views of an old woman carrying her burden-basket, as well as several images showing elderly Indian men dressed in varied combinations of native and white-men's clothing. These photographs were unfortunately similar to many images of reservation life taken by other photographers, showing the declining Native American civilization. She made very little attempt to pose her subjects, and certainly did not do so in the manner common to her earlier, heroic photographs. In November, 1917, while on a picture-taking expedition to the Weitchpec area, Emma broke her arm in a severe fall. Fractured in two places, the bone failed at first to heal properly, and had to be rebroken and reset.

Despite a period of intense pain from this injury, Emma secured a commission to provide the government with construction and launching photographs of a series of wooden vessels that were being constructed at the nearby Rolph Shipyards to serve as transports for wartime cargo. To help her in this task, she purchased a panoramic camera capable of taking photographic views as long as 12 feet. With traditional 6½- x 8½- and 8- x 10-inch format cameras, as well as with the panoramic camera, she photographed the completion and subsequent launch of the first wooden ship to be produced locally as part of the Navy's war transport program.

The effects of the war on the nation's economy could not be restrained forever, and by 1918, "belt tightening" became a patriotic principle among those supporting the military effort. As the Army's need for additional funds became more acute, the Liberty Bond and War Stamp programs also grew. At this point, Emma's Klamath Princess, Ah-tra-ah-saun, reappeared in public with her husband known as Chief White Elk: *... FAMOUS CHEROKEE CHIEF AND AMERICAN SOLDIER MAKES HIT ... APPEARS IN FULL FEATHERED PANOPLY OF TRIBE WITH KLAMATH PRINCESS BRIDE IN BOND CAMPAIGN.*

Whether White Elk was in fact a chief, or even a Cherokee, may

(photograph opposite) Bertha Thompson and her husband Chief White Elk.

well be debated. He could sing and recite well, however, and bond subscriptions poured in following his public performances. His most popular program included such diverse fare as renditions of *"Joan of Arc," "A Perfect Day," "Mother Machree," "Le Marsaillaise,"* and songs and stories of the war zone. Emma made a number of photographs of the couple in their Indian regalia and may well have been instrumental in arranging their patriotic participation in the local Liberty Bond drive.

In June, 1918, Emma photographed William Jennings Bryan, whose "Cross of Gold" oratory had made him a three-time candidate for the United States Presidency. Upon his arrival in Eureka on a Sunday afternoon, Bryan proceeded directly to the Freeman Art Studio to have his portrait taken. Finished prints were delivered the same afternoon. A short time later, James Rolph, Jr., who was a candidate for governor of California, sat for his official portrait at the studio. It had also become voguish for prominent members of society to have their portraits taken by the illustrious Emma B. Freeman.

Pleased with her successes in Eureka, and at the height of her career, Emma decided to return to San Francisco. In past years she had departed from that city in despair, and had returned there in both scandal and victory. San Francisco still shone as a lodestar of opportunity to Emma. She obtained a ten-year lease on a building in the fashionable Sutter Street area. Under the direction of Harvey Burnett, the renovation of the new store progressed quickly. A factory on Eddy Street to mould picture frames and other curios was ready for the public at about the same time. Emma opened the doors of her San Francisco Art Company store in May, 1919.

Several hundred people attended the gala event, which lasted from early afternoon until midnight. Emma Freeman and Harvey Burnett were on hand to receive guests and to provide tours of their newly remodeled, three-story, fireproof building. The main floor of the store measured 40 x 60 feet and was devoted to a large display of art goods. Many of these items had been produced in the Eddy Street factory and were made of a product which Emma had patented, called "Freeman Metalboard." While the exact origin of this material is unclear, the *Humboldt Standard* gave it a good report:

*Her [Emma's] latest stunt is the invention of a new composition . . . designed to take the place of plaster-of-Paris and other*

68

*brittle materials now used in the manufacture of picture frames, mouldings, statuettes, and bas-relief . . . All who have seen Emma B. Freeman's metal board are enthusiastic in their praise, not only in regard to the remarkable results she has obtained in imitating metals, but in the artistic manner in which she has sculptured her work.*

**(Humboldt Standard, June 25, 1918)**

The second floor of the new Freeman Art Company — known as the Humboldt County Room — featured Indian baskets, artifacts, photographs, and paintings from the Northcoast area. The third and final floor contained Emma's portrait studio, described by many as among the finest in the city. Each of the rooms was furnished with specially-made furniture, upholstered in green damask, and the walls were appointed with matching drapery. The store's woodwork was finished elegantly in old English ivory with grey paneling. An indirect lighting system had been installed to give the interior a rainbow effect when viewed from outside during evening hours.

Among Emma's first clients was the prestigious firm of I. Magnin and Company. They sent their new fashion designs and gowns for Emma to photograph, using live models. Her photographs were intended for use both in the salon's advertising promotion and as a visual record of their creations. Since Fred Chamley had remained in Eureka to manage that city's store, Emma had to oversee all aspects of the studio's operations. Burnett split his time between operation of the salesroom and the management of the Eddy Street factory.

For the first time in many years, Emma did not reside at her place of work. She lived, instead, in a nearby guesthouse, but soon found herself spending little time there. The store and studio increasingly demanded her attention. She also found photographic competition in San Francisco fierce, with more than 90 firms striving for commissions. In addition, nearly 50 stores offered the kind of art supplies available from the Freeman Art Company.

In a short time, the enterprise drained all of Emma's financial reserves. She had also exhausted her credit with commercial banks. The firm continued in business only through the sheer determination of Emma Freeman and Burnett to recruit new clients while accomplishing the tasks already underway.

In the end, even determination was not equal to the task at hand. An ambitious undertaking in all respects, the new Freeman Art Company required huge quantities of money to meet obligations and

**Fashion illustration from the San Francisco Chronicle at the time of Emma's re-entry into the cosmopolitan scene.**

*Courtesy of I. Magnin & Co.*

to continue operation. In desperation, Emma sold the Eureka store to provide additional capital. Although she was a dynamo of energy, the tasks she was called upon to perform multiplied, and she began to suffer from periods of sickness and generally poor health.

In this time of difficulty, the *San Francisco Examiner* wrote a story headlined, *"PLOT TO LOOT TURK TEMPLE CHARGED HERE."* The accompanying article linked Harvey Burnett with a bizarre plot to buy rugs and art goods from a Turkish rug merchant named Obadia Nathan. With purported financing through Burnett, Nathan was supposed to have proceeded to Constantinople to steal rugs, artifacts, and the like from an Islamic temple, smuggling them later into the United States. The Freeman Art Company was named as the final destination of the pilfered items. Caught in the bad publicity surrounding Burnett's alleged actions, Emma watched with dismay as her sales began to fall. The suit was settled out of court but the reputation of the Freeman Art Company was badly damaged.

The company incorporated in 1922 with Emma as President and Burnett as Vice-president, seeking additional capital from stockholders. The firm moved soon after to a location with reduced overhead, but even so it was unable to meet its now-long list of debts. On August 10, 1923, the *San Francisco Examiner* noted in an announcement *"ARTIST FAILS FOR $15,000"*:

*Enumerating among her assets six paint brushes worth $2, with which she had apparently painted a picture of debts aggregating $15,155.35, Emma B. Freeman yesterday filed a voluntary petition in bankruptcy. She is the proprietor of the Freeman Art Company . . .*

*Mrs. Freeman, whose famous photograph of California Redwoods, taken near Eureka, was presented to President Harding and hangs at the present time in the White House at Washington, enumerated assets of $159.*

*These included a sewing machine worth $7, furniture valued at $100, clothes at $50, and a half dozen paint brushes above mentioned, which caused all the trouble.*

**(San Francisco Examiner, August 10, 1923)**

Emma B. Freeman doggedly salvaged what assets were available, called on those who remembered her artistic accomplishments, and started again. In 1924, she was listed in the *San Francisco Business Directory* as proprietor of an art goods shop on Jones Street. By

71

1925, the listing had changed to include a partner, but Emma was no longer operating as a creative artist. Stripped of her studio, she neglected her painting, drawing, and photography. Lonely and despairing, she finally gave up her shop.

On September 4, 1925, at the age of 45, Emma suddenly remarried. Her husband was a 60-year-old bookkeeper for the Shell Oil Company named Edward Blake. Born in South Australia to Irish and English parents, Blake had never before been married. After a honeymoon that included a visit to Humboldt County, the Blakes lived quietly on Castenada Street in San Francisco. There, on Christmas Eve in 1927, Emma suffered a severe stroke. She lingered with its effects until March 26, when she died at the age of 48.

Her life, marked by loyalty to an intense personal expression, had also been a voyage of self-discovery. Schooled as an artist, she became an accidental photographer. A farmgirl who pined for the art mecca of San Francisco, she did her most creative work in the unsophisticated backwoods. Her artistic output, like the history of the Northern California Indians, was largely ignored until recently. Now both remain a basis for legend.

# Portfolio

## 107 ANCIENT LAW

*A characteristic full blooded Klamath native, garbed in the blankets and holding the forked stick — the symbol of authority — also used in locating hidden springs and always in evidence at ceremonial tribe rites. Health, strength, youth and vigor all bend to the authority of the man with the forked stick.*

### 119   AH-TRA-AH-SAUN

*Meaning "Valley of the Mountain."*
*This little Indian maiden was*
*selected to lead the procession*
*at the opening of the great San*
*Francisco Exposition. Dressed as*
*in this picture, in native garb of*
*skins, beads, shells, carved orna-*
*ments and native gold trinkets and*
*holding the woven basket of her*
*family's lineage, she makes an*
*interesting portrait.*

### 148   IN THE EVENING SHADOWS

*Sitting where the evening sun has
painted the vistas of distant hills.
To you, lonesome, but to an Indian,
the chirp of the cricket, the evening whistle of the whip-poor-will or
the lark calling its mate, is story
and song and happiness. Civilization to an Indian is noise, unrest
and friction. Who will say they are
wrong? This Indian girl says she is
happy.*

### 101 WEAVER OF DREAMS

*At the feet of an Indian maiden are
scores of baskets, treasured
because woven by those who have
passed into the shadows. These baskets
tell stories in the patterns of the
weaving. It is an art in which the
Klamath tribe probably excel all
other Indian weavers — the basket
she holds is unfinished, the hands
that have worked at it have been
stayed by the Great Spirit.*

## 102   CALL OF THE BLOOD

*It has been rightly declared that
"an Indian never forgets." This
girl clothed in the raiment of her
people is watching thru a lighted
window an enemy of her tribe. One
more look, then back where counsel
will be taken. Falsehood and dishon-
esty find no lodging place in the
people of the hills. She is on the
invisible line between forest pride
and modern civilization.*

83

Title Unknown

## 115 DAUGHTER OF THE KLAMATH

*A full-blooded Klamath woman of thirty years of age. Study the wealth of rich, raven hair — not an unusual feature, but almost general among the people of her tribe. The high cheek bones, the broad nose, the firm mouth mark the characteristics of the people that are passing and some day will be only memory.*

Title Unknown

89

*117  WEST WAYS*

*An Indian maiden, at the water's
edge with bow and arrow, across the
water the distant low-lying hills,
at her feet a mound of wild ferns
and arbutus. Standing silhouetted
against the sky, she is a statue of
youthful strength, beauty and charm.
She is wearing the white feather of
an unmarried girl.*

### 123  ALLEGIANCE

*An Indian girl's face of enchanting beauty. She has just taken an oath of obedience and loyalty and turns to ponder on the deeper meaning of it all. She wears the head band of the "Hoopa' tribe with the white feather of an unmarried maiden.*

142    SHASTA DAISY

*Science took the little flower of the prairie and improved it and science has also taken the Indian girls and taught them ideas of culture in thought, dress and mode of living. This picture is of an Indian girl returned to her people from studies completed. A touch of the old life in dress but the increased intelligence of education is in her face. This picture shows Mount Shasta in the distance.*

95

Title Unknown

## 116   GODDESS OF THE FEAST

*An Indian maiden appointed by her people to prepare the "acorn soup" for the event. Strange as it may seem, these splendid baskets, such as she holds, are so closely woven that they retain liquids. The cooking is done by heated stones placed in the foods. It is a charming picture of lights and shadows.*

Title Unknown

Emma B. Freeman
Northern Calif. Indian Series.
Copy - 1915

## 145   IN THE LAND OF THE SETTING SUN

*A day spent with his bow. It is now*
*the hour when the sun is setting.*
*No game has come to his hand — it*
*is a day lost. Marvelous strength*
*and health are his, he turns his*
*back to the sinking sun toward the*
*east with a resolve for greater*
*energies on the morrow.*

## 134 CHILDHOOD RECOLLECTIONS

*An Indian maiden has stolen away to take one more look into the pool where she sees mirrored her face. Tomorrow she moves deeper into the forests. Behind her are the mute evidences of white man's coming. A man made fence and the telegraph; fields are planted, civilization has encroached. "It was not so when I played here as a child."*

# Catalogue of Native American Images

*exhibited at the Panama-Pacific International Exposition

A — The Edward E. Ayer Collection, The Newberry Library

B — California State Library, California Collection

C — Other Sources

114 AH-PURA-AH-WAY
*(Klamath Worship, see also Oh-Pura-Ah-Way),*
Yurok, 1914-15: ABC

*119 AH-TRA-AH-SAUN
*(Valley of the Mountain, see also Princess Ah-Tra-Ah-Saun),* Bertha Thompson, Yurok, December 3, 1914: ABC

*123 ALLEGIANCE
Vivian Chase(?), Hupa 1914-15: ABC

146 ALONE
Bertha Stevens, Yurok, 1915: A

*107 ANCIENT LAW
Robert Spott, Yurok 1914-15: ABC

*136 AUTUMN OF
THE KLAMATH

*128 BARTERED BRIDE, THE
1914-15: B

BASKET MAKER,
Hand-painted version reproduced in black and white, Hazel Ferris(?), 1915: C

107

*138 BATHED IN
SUNLIGHT FLOOD
1914-15: AC

Cleveland, Jessie(?), leather
jerkin and headband, 1915-16:
A

*102 CALL OF BLOOD
Hupa, 1914-15: AB

Cleveland, Jessie(?), leather
jerkin and headband, 1915-16:
A

106 CALL OF THE PAST
*(The Half-breed Girl, see also
Out of the Past),*
Vivian Chase(?), Hupa, 1914-
15: ABC; Painted version: B

Cleveland, Jessie(?), headband
with feather, 1915-16: A

*121 CALL OF THE WILD
Bertha Thompson, Yurok,
1914: ABC

163 CLIMBER, THE
Bertha Stevens, Yurok 1914-
15: ABC

*134 CHILDHOOD
RECOLLECTIONS
Grace Wayman, Yurok,
1914-15: AC

210
Couple, Bertha Thompson and
Chief White Elk, 1918: AC

Cleveland, Jessie(?), leather
jerkin and basket hat,
1915-16: AC

COURIER, THE

Dancer, White Deerskin, 1916:
C

Dancer, White Deerskin, 1916:
C

Female, unidentified, basket
maker, 1915: A

Female, unidentified, Beaded
headband, 1915-16: A

Female, unidentified, elderly,
1915-16: A

Female, unidentified, elderly,
1915-16: A

Female, unidentified, elderly,
basket hat, 1915-16: A

 Female, unidentified, elderly, carrying basket, 1917-18: A

 Female, unidentified, feather, bead necklace, 1915: C

 Female, unidentified, elderly, carrying basket, 1917-18: A

 Female, unidentified, "Indian Head" portrait, 1915: C

 Female, unidentified, elderly, carrying basket, 1917-18: A

 Female, unidentified, "Indian Head" before vignetting, 1915: C

 Female, unidentified, headband with feather, 1914-15: A

 Female, unidentified, making baskets outdoors, 1915-16: A

 Female, unidentified, headband with feather, 1914-15: A

 Ferris, Hazel(?), portrait with necklace, 1915: A

 Female, unidentified, feather, bead necklace, 1915: C

 Ferris, Hazel(?), portrait with necklace, 1915: A

Ferris, Hazel(?), portrait with necklace, 1915: A

Group, unidentified, White deerskin dance, 1916: AC

Ferris, Hazel(?), portrait with necklace, 1915: A

Group, unidentified, White deerskin dance, 1916: AC

*105 FIVE GENERA-TIONS
Yurok, 1914-15: ABC

Group, Bertha Thompson, Bertha Stevens, Chief White Elk, 1918: C

Freeman, Emma B., Indian garb, self-portrait(?), 1915-16: C

*122 HEART OF NATURE
Hupa, 1914-15: ABC

*133 HUMBOLDT WINNOW BASKET
Hupa, 1914-15: AC

*116 GODDESS OF THE FEAST
Hupa, 1914-15: ABC

*108 IAQUA
*(meaning salutation)*,
Hupa, 1914-15: A

*104 GOLDEN WEST
Hupa, 1914-15: AB

INDIAN MAIDS
INVOCATION

111

Indian stick game, (attributed), 1917-18: C

LAST TRAIL, THE
Bertha Thompson(?), Yurok, 1914-15: BC

148 IN THE EVENING
SHADOWS
Grace Wayman, Yurok, 1915: AB

*126 LITTLE PROVIDER
Bertha Stevens, Yurok, 1914-15: AB

*111 IN THE LAND OF
SKY BLUE WATERS
Hupa, 1914-15: A

*125 LOST TRAIL, THE

*109 IN THE LAND
OF THE GODS

141 MADONNA OF THE
INDIANS, THE
*(see also Romance),*
Hazel Ferris(?), Yurok, 1914-15: AB

*145 IN THE LAND OF
THE SETTING SUN
Robert Spott, Yurok, 1914-15: AC

*143 MAID OF LEGENDS
Vivian Chase(?), Hupa, 1914-15: AB

KLAMATH SAM

Klamath sweathouse, (attributed), 1917-18: A

Male, elderly, called "Dandy Bill", 1915-16: A

KLAMATH TANGO

112

 Male, unidentified, bow and arrows, 1914-15: C

 Male, unidentified, feathered headdress, 1915: A

 Male, unidentified, holding cermonial obsidian blade, 1915-16: A

 Male, unidentified, headdress, bow and arrows, 1914-15: A

 Male, unidentified, European(?), with bow and arrows, 1915: AC

 Male, unidentified, headdress, necklace over trousers, 1915-16: C

 Male, unidentified, European(?), with bow and arrows, 1915: A

 Male, unidentified, woodpecker headdress and shell necklace, 1915-16: A

 Male, unidentified, examining necklace, 1915: A

 Male, unidentified, woodpecker headdress, 1915-16: A

 Male, unidentified, examining necklace, 1915: A

 Male, unidentified, woodpecker headdress, 1915-16: A

113

Male, unidentified, wood-pecker headdress, 1915-16: A

Male, unidentified, wood-pecker headdress, 1915-16: A

Pearch, Ed.(?), cloth headband with feathers, 1915-16: A

MESSAGE OF THE GREAT SPIRIT

Pearch, Ed.(?), cloth headband with feathers, 1915-16: A

Pearch, Ed.(?), cloth headband with feathers, 1915-16: A

Pearch, Ed.(?), cloth headband with feathers, 1915-16: A

154 PRINCESS TA-WA-NA
Yurok, 1914-15: A

Scene, Indian school children and maypole, (attributed), Hupa, 1915: C

SHADOWS

*113 RED ARROW

*139 RED MAN'S DREAM
Hupa, 1914-15: AB

*142 SHASTA DAISY
Vivian Chase(?), Hupa, 1914-15: AB

*137 SNOW DEER

*135 REFLECTIONS
Grace Wayman, Yurok, 1914-15: AB

*132 SOLITUDE

Spott, Robert, modeling ceremonial costume, Yurok, 1915-16: A

*120 REMINISCENCE
*(or Reminiscent),*
Vivian Chase(?), Hupa 1914-15: AB

Spott, Robert, modeling ceremonial costume, Yurok, 1915-16: A

*141 ROMANCE
*(see also Madonna of the Indians)*

Scene, Indian dugout on Klamath River, (attributed), hand painted by Bertha Stevens, 1915-16: C

Spott, Robert, modeling ceremonial costume, Yurok, 1915-16: A

Spott, Robert, modeling ceremonial costume, Yurok, 1915-16: A

Spott, Robert, White deerskin costume, Yurok, 1915-16: A

Wayman, Grace, fringed jerkin, Yurok, 1915: C

Spott, Robert, with dugout canoe, Yurok, 1915: AC

Wayman, Grace, with unfinished basket, Yurok, 1915: C

Spott, Robert, with dugout canoe, with white man, Yurok, 1915-16: A

Wayman, Grace, with unfinished basket, Yurok, 1915: C

Spott, Robert, with dugout canoe, white man cropped, Yurok, 1915-16: A

Wayman, Grace, with unfinished basket, Yurok, 1915: C

Thompson, Bertha, "Indian Head" portrait, Yurok 1915: B

*117 WEST WAYS
Yurok, 1914-15: AB

*130 WINTER GARDEN
Hupa, 1914-15: AB

*131 YESTERTHOUGHTS
1914-15: B

## BIBLIOGRAPHY OF BOOKS
## AND PERIODICALS WHICH
## INCLUDE EXAMPLES OF
## EMMA B. FREEMAN'S PHOTOGRAPHS

### *BOOKS*

Dolezal, Robert J. *Exploring Redwood National Park;* p44. Eureka: Interface California Corporation, 1974.

. . . Native American portraits . . .

Ward, Charles Willis. *Humboldt County California;* p65,73,77,95. Eureka: Chamber of Commerce, 1915.

. . . Native American studio and outdoor portraits . . .

### *MAGAZINES AND NEWSPAPERS*

Anon. *Humboldt Standard.* "Humboldt County 100,000 Population Edition"; p14. Eureka: April 2, 1917.

. . . shipbuilding, Rolph shipyard . . .

Anon. *Humboldt Standard.* p6. Eureka: August 2, 1918.

. . . portrait of James Rolph, Jr. candidate for Governor of California . . .

Anon. *Humboldt Times.* "Get Acquainted Edition"; p2-8. Eureka: March 31, 1916.

. . . numerous commercial (Freeman Art Company) portraits of civic and community leaders . . .

Anon. *Illustrated Review.* vol. IV, No. 19; p14-17. Atascadero: March 1918.

. . . four pages Native American portraits, mostly Emma's . . .

Anon. *Recreation & Outdoor World;* cover. New York: August 1914.

. . . portrait of Miss Ward . . .

Anon.* *San Francisco Argonaut.* "Christmas Edition"; p unknown. San Francisco: 1918.

. . . artistic portraits . . .

Anon. *San Francisco Chronicle.* "Royal Indian maid in today's parade will lead native daughter's column; honor for Princess Ah-Tra-Ah-Saun"; p1. San Francisco: February 20, 1915.

. . . Native American portraits . . .

Anon. *San Francisco Chronicle.* "First pictures of stranded cruiser Milwaukee with work of rescuing her crew in progress"; p . San Francisco: January 15, 1917.

. . . shipwreck images . . .

Anon. *Studio Light;* p2,5,7,9,11,13,16,17, 19,21, Rochester: June 1915.

. . .artistic portraiture . . .

Field, Charles K. editor. *Sunset; the Pacific monthly.* "Across the editor's desk". vol. XXXVIII, No. 2; p6. San Francisco: February 1917.

. . . Native American portrait . . .

Frear, Frances. *Leslie's Illustrated Weekly Newspaper.* "In the world of womankind"; New York: January 14, 1915.

. . . Native American portrait . . .

Freeman, Emma B. *A catalog of pictures from the Camera and Brush of Emma B. Freeman (Northern California Indian Artist);* Eureka: 1915.

. . . Native American portrait plus catalogue listings of images displayed at the Panama-Pacific International Exposition in 1915.

*unable to locate extant example

Freeman, Emma B. *Pacific Outdoors.* "With Nature's Children"; p197. New York: October, 1917.

. . . Native American portraits . . .

Grant, Madison. *Zoological Society Bulletin.* "Saving the Redwoods"; p90,96,98,100, 102,104,106,108,117. New York: September 1919.

. . . typical commercial (Freeman Art Company) images showing the majesty of the redwood region and the threat of man to this environment . . .

Putnam, Edna Hildebrand. *The Overland Monthly.* "Ah-Pura-Way the dance of the white deer skin and other Klamath worship dances". Vol. LXIX, No. 4; p276-283. San Francisco: April 1917.

. . . Native American dance costume studies . . .

Wog, N. A. *Camera Craft.* "An artist with the camera". Vol. XXIV; p189-192. San Francisco: May 1917.

. . . artistic portraits . . .

# Appendix A

## Women's Work: Women and the Arts in Rural Humboldt County, 1900-1920

Living in the remote northern reaches of California in the first decade of the Twentieth Century, Emma Freeman suffered under a dual handicap — she was a woman and an artist. Her success and recognition were even more significant when one considers the stultifying restraints of a male-dominated region whose artists' endeavors were largely ignored by the outside world. At the same time, these factors may account for Emma's relative obscurity to this day.

Throughout the period that Emma worked, the popular convention remained that a woman's place is in the home. Although the international struggle to achieve women's suffrage was already a half-century old, women still had little place in professional life (nor did they get the vote until 1920, eight years before Emma's death).

Historically, women found it difficult to become merchants or traders, for legal restrictions forbade most women the right to inherit or own property. Among the few roles in which women found acceptance were those of the teacher and governess. These offered quasi-respectable alternatives for women of good character who lacked financial security or a "suitable" husband, but they provided horribly low pay.

However, the edifice of traditional male and female roles continued to crumble as the Twentieth Century opened. Women's rights was a hotly-contested issue. Even in Humboldt County, California, the feminist onslaught produced such anguished editorials as these:

*WHERE WILL WOMAN STOP? ... It is less than 50 years since American girls were refused admission to the colleges their brothers attended. Now there are more women in the colleges than men. Almost every agency of modern times caters to woman. Merchants vie for her custom. The pulpit wants her strong support. The press seeks her favor and patronage. Woman is no longer behind the throne, she is the throne ... All this change of a few years seems a radical*

Why cannot woman be satisfied with her present position which her present rights assign her? Do not the men see to her safety and comfort? But her present right was donated and dictated to her, not created and achieved by her. She was granted just the measure of freedom that man considered desirable for her on his account. Man created right — changed, limited, extended right — interpreted and applied right to women. But woman, to be a self, must participate in the formation of her rights. And as to women's comfort and safety, these cannot take the place of freedom! Even poodles are comfortable and safe, contented and happy; but they are not free, and have no dream of freedom. Trouble, and struggle, and sorrow, nay, danger and loss and the risk of ruin for woman, as for man, with freedom, are far better and nobler than imperturbability and repose and protection without freedom. The point is that woman can no longer allow any sort of disqualification or disability that is contary to selfhood. The point is that the free unfolding of personality is the most necessary thing that there is in the world for either man or woman.

(The Forum Magazine, July, 1914)

departure. But cast your eyes over Europe.

-The women of Britain are pounding on the doors of parliament seeking suffrage.

-In Germany the gates of ancient universities have been lifted from their hinges to let women in.

-In Italy the parliament has appointed a commission . . . for equal suffrage.

-The French women have gone ahead of men in the field of scientific discovery. And in England of the 12 best selling books every one was written by a woman.

-Even in darkest Russia women physicians are teaching the doctors of the world advanced methods of hospital work.

-But most striking of all in Finland — think of it — in Finland — 10 women now occupy seats as law makers in the legislature of that duchy!

-This is the woman's age . . . In this new equation of modern life is man to be the X . . . The unknown quantity?

(Humboldt Times, 19 May 1907)

Local newspapers also chronicled the incursion of women into roles formerly held by men. Headlines of the time, written by men, include: *"WOMEN TO RUN STREETCARS"; "FIRST WOMAN ON A JURY"; "WOMAN FARMER RAISES RECORD CROP"; "EIGHT WOMEN CANDIDATES FOR PUBLIC OFFICE."*

Humboldt County did recognize competence and industry as important personal traits. However, a women's accomplishment in a traditionally male endeavor often was heralded as an oddity, though it might receive a small measure of grudging admiration:

### WOMAN BUILDER OF HER HOME

*It is a two story house containing seven rooms . . . The house was erected by Mrs. Edna Rhyne . . . she laid all the heavy beams, erected the studding, put up the walls, shingled the roof, prepared the inside casings for doors and windows . . . there are no rough edges and a trip into the parlor makes one wonder how it was all done by a woman.*

(Humboldt Times, 26 March 1907)

Conceding some ground to the feminists, the male establishment cast around for an acceptable mode of expression for women that did not erode the masculine framework of local society. One editorial titled *"WORK FOR EUREKA'S WOMEN"* offered the following advice:

*[What] Eureka needs now is a big, active, thoroughly organized women's club that will undertake agitation looking to the beautification of streets, the improvement of sidewalks and crossings, the boulevarding of certain thoroughfares, the adornment of school grounds so bleak and uninviting, the preservation*

*of those natural beauty spots in and around the city that have been spared by the woodsman — encouraging the abolishment of unsightly fences and sign boards, and the like.*

*... The uncouth hand of man scars and gnashes the beautiful face of nature in Humboldt, oft-times, but the smooth and gentle hand of woman can touch the wound and and heal them.*

(Humboldt Times, 26 Feb 1907)

Six years later, it could be seen from the local paper that women had steadily shifted into the relatively menial jobs that had increased as a result of the burgeoning American economy. The tone of the following editorial implied that women should not only be thankful for these developments but also forsake efforts at further progress.

*Two inventions of the last generation have given employment to a vast army of young women — the typewriter and the telephone. There are more than one hundred thousand women engaged in stenography. More than a fourth of that number are at work in telephone offices. Many thousand women are clerks ... there are more than a tenth of a million women nurses in the United States.*

*A multitude of women — almost a third of a million — are teaching schools, painting, or music. When it is remembered that there are only 155,000 housekeepers in the country and only a million servants and waiters — including both men and women — it will be seen that a large proportion of women are entering the higher walks, so called.*

(Humboldt Times, 27 Feb 1913)

A major milestone on the path to women's rights was the outbreak of World War I. Working women suddenly became an integral part of the nation's war effort. By 1916 the *Humboldt Times* evidenced a somewhat more favorable attitude, if grudging and still condescending, in a progress report on *"Women's Work."*

*... While the old saying that a Woman's Place Is In The Home still holds true, that Place is no longer a mere dispensary to provide the material needs of the household, but the throneroom where the beneficent power of enlightened Womanhood throws its influence beyond the narrow confines of the family circle.*

*While masculine and feminine opinions may differ in regard to the proper attention of womankind in the political world, the strides in questions of education and political and domestic economy made by women in the past few years has given them a new station in the world's work from which no amount of diverging opinion can dislodge them.*

(Humboldt Times, 15 July 1916)

121

As the war progressed, women became involved in almost all aspects of the effort — Emma Freeman even volunteered to photograph at the front, after winning her spurs as a photojournalist when she photographed a naval disaster near Humboldt Bay in early 1917.

By war's end, the *Humboldt Times* was forced to concede that women had *"vindicated their contentions that they were eminently capable of performing the tasks of men from the menial to the executive."*

But strangely, during this time of loosening male control of women, many of the artists of the day remained fixated on the traditional female image (though Emma went so far as to pose an Indian woman with a warrior's bow and arrows). Another local publication, the *Humboldt Standard*, presented this survey in an editorial entitled *"ART AND THE NEW WOMAN"*:

*Seventy-seven pictures at the spring exhibition of the National Academy of Design are of women. Seventeen of the pictured ladies sit with idle hands. Nine of them are sewing, most of them in casual fashion devoid of serious purpose. Five read. Five are accompanied by babies. Two play instruments, one eats, one writes, one is in bed, three in gardens, one at market.*

*Feminism — or at least that phase of it which expects a woman to be busied at productive work, seems to have run ahead of art. According to the painters, the chief concerns of women seem to be reading, sewing and dressing, with the emphasis in the latter of putting a rose in the hair. The woman who has made the analysis says, "for our part, it is years since we have seen a woman with a rose in her hair; yet each academy sees renewed eloquent testimony that women still spend vast amounts of time putting one there."*

**(Humboldt Standard, 27 April 1915)**

Questions regarding the status of the fine arts go quite beyond the depiction of women. For many years, and persisting perhaps to this day, artists working in Northwestern California have worked in undeserved anonymity. They were hamstrung in two significant ways — their own difficulties in capturing the majestic yet evanescent redwood country and the so-called art world's blindness to the area north of San Francisco.

San Francisco was indeed the northernmost bastion of the creative arts in the West at the turn of the century. But artists like Emma Freeman were busily at work in the more than 300-mile-long stretch between that city and the Oregon border. Proof of this came in a landmark exhibition held in San Francisco in 1915.

The Panama-Pacific International Exposition may have been the first serious and effective attempt to reveal the scope of the arts of the Pacific West. Earlier exhibitions, such as the San Francisco Mechanic's Fair of 1894, had included galleries devoted to the fine arts, but their main emphasis had been on technology and agriculture. Many smaller exhibitions had featured regional artworks, but generally these shows had gone unheralded beyond their immediate locale.

In contrast, the Panama-Pacific International Exposition brought together the finest art of the West and displayed it along with the best that the world could provide. Gallery patrons could finally compare a substantial selection of fine art from Arizona, New Mexico and California with examples from Europe and the Americas.

Regional pride, enthusiasm and momentum galvanized connoisseurs, critics and artists alike. Art became the social topic of the day. Critic Porter Garnett, writing in 1916, commented:

*It would be well, therefore, to admit at once that, whatever local pride may prompt some to say, California is both too young and too remote to have produced very much art of a high order . . .*

*Now, while California has undoubtedly produced art, she has not produced AN art; that is to say, there is not yet an art that is characteristically Californian and at the same time universal . . .*

*Before a country or a community can be said to have produced an art of its own, its artist must show a native strain in their work . . . they may — and many do — REPRESENT California, but how many of them EXPRESS California? . . .*

(California's Magazine, 1916)

The same magazine carried a partial rejoinder from Michael Williams in an article entitled *"The Pageant of Californian Art."*

*First then, it is obvious, even unto triteness, that the circumstances which so strongly distinguish California and give her a place dramatically apart from her sister states, may be summed up in three master words, namely, beauty, romance, and youth . . . which express the character of the state.*

(California's Magazine, 1916)

Even if these distinguishing features are accepted, other differences exist between art originating in Southern California and art from the North of the state. Even in the North it is true to say that, since variations in landform affect the landscape artist, the further north the artist works the more he differs in his mode of expression.

Moving northward from the San Francisco Bay region the terrain changes from rolling hills into oak and scrub-covered ridges. There are more rivers and streams, the coastline is rugged, with precipitous headlands. The mountains are more pronounced and the trees and other flora increase in luxuriance, creating huge forests, closing off the vistas, and giving all a sense of wilderness and isolation.

This perception of isolation and proximity to nature was clearly evident in the Panama-Pacific International Exposition exhibit produced by artists and craftsmen from the Humboldt County region:

*Humboldt County's display was unique in that it had brought to the Exposition two great sections of a giant redwood tree. These sections were made into rooms, one of which housed the display of redwood. Here were hung the beautiful paintings picturing the famous forests of Humboldt. The ceiling of the room, which was twenty feet in diameter, was made of polished, hand-carved redwood. In the center was suspended a crystal candelabra which reflected its light upon the highly polished surface of the wood furnishings.*

*Paintings were framed in redwood burl . . . Every article made of burl was highly polished and is most artistic. In the center of the room stood one of the most noteworthy and costly tables in the Exposition. This is made of a single slab of redwood burl, is seven feet in diameter, without a flaw . . .*

(California's Magazine, 1916)

The raw power of frontier Humboldt County overwhelmed the timid and challenged the bold. What sculptor could create a work more inspired and more revealing than that which nature had already provided? What muralist could create a panorama more exciting than that feeling of endless distance which is to be seen from a coastal headland? What architect could provide a habitation more powerful than that of a sunlit redwood forest?

Evidence that the Humboldt County region intimidated the artists of the period is clearly shown in canvases produced by local landscape painters. Trees seemed too huge, waterways too expansive and the ocean too turbulent to compress into the frozen confines of the artist's canvas. C. T. Wilson, famous as a painter of the redwoods, came to Humboldt County in the 1890's from Guatemala, intrigued by stories of the sailors of the lumber fleet. Until his departure in 1916, he specialized in paintings featuring the California redwoods, several of which were exhibited at the Panama-Pacific International Exposition. His works were often large; the largest was designed to wrap 98 feet around the walls of a lavish library.

Wilson's heavy oils of the towering redwood forests reflect the mysterious and the formidable. He admitted that he often experienced deep frustration in his efforts to capture them on canvas:

*. . . not in an hour nor a day nor a year was this wonderful transmutation to be accomplished. Nature was ever fickle, the countless wonders of the forest varied with every sunbeam, the aisles of shade became aisles of light, and sunshine and shadow tantalized the artist who sought to imprison them in oil and preserve them . . .*

(Humboldt Standard, May 2, 1916)

(photograph opposite) A Martella Cone Lane oil painting of Humboldt County redwoods which was exhibited at the Panama-Pacific International Exposition in 1915.

Artists linked to the Humboldt County region were few, although many visited the area to set up their easels. The ranks of landscape painters from 1900 to World War I include a small but persistent group of women. Several of these deserve special mention.

Property of Humboldt County

125

Cora B. Wright (1886-1948) started painting in Martinez, California after a period of formal training from Manuel Valencia. After her marriage she moved with her husband to Eureka and worked actively, painting Humboldt County vistas and studio still-lifes until 1946. She was a good friend of C. T. Wilson, and painted many views of the redwoods as well as scenes along the Klamath River.

Martella Cone Lane (1879-1962), the daughter of portrait painter Lydia Cone, studied under landscape artists William Keith, Franz A. Bischoff, and John Marshall Gamble. She was an active California landscape artist well before 1900 and featured the redwoods in many of her works. Like Wilson and Wright, she exhibited at the Panama-Pacific International Exposition. Actively engaged in the study and teaching of art for many decades, she later became Dean of Art at Chapman College.

Also active in the period were Mrs. Deedie (Thompson) Bland, who painted farm and orchard landscapes of the Eel River Valley. A later arrival was professional artist Mary (Minnie) Steinhauer, who became a close associate of Emma B. Freeman.

Emma's contribution to the Panama-Pacific International Exposition received wide acclaim at the time, but did not aid in the search for a definition of so-called "Redwoods School" of art. She had worked outside the mainstreams of both art and photography and, as a businesswoman, had experienced the added difficulty of functioning in a man's world. Being a woman and an artist in a rough land and in a rugged male culture presented grave obstacles, yet her work remarkably endures.

# Appendix B
## Indian Customs and White Exploitation: a Northwestern California Summary

The Northwest California coast provided a home for several small tribes of America's first residents, known today as the Yurok, Wiyot, Karok, Tolowa, Chilula, and Hupa Indians. Despite their close physical proximity, these tribal families exhibited separate cultures and languages. In early times, however, the divisions between these tribal or cultural groupings were not clearly recognized; the natives identified with their village of origin rather than any tribal affiliation.

Living between the present-day city of Eureka and the Oregon border, these Native Americans occupied the coastal beaches and inland waterways of a spectacularly scenic region which is bigger than Rhode Island. Vast redwood groves, dense and forbidding, and nurtured by damp fog and extended rainy seasons, stretched inland from the sea. Many rivers and streams traversed the area, providing pathways through precipitous mountain ranges. Indian villages were frequently located on the banks of larger streams or adjacent to the seacoast, where fish, mollusks and other foodstuffs were plentiful.

For the most part peaceful relations existed among these native townsites. Despite linguistic and religious differences, trading and other contacts between groups was commonplace. The greatest source of disputes involved individual honor. The individual or his family group controlled hunting and fishing rights in specified areas. When these rights were violated complex fines were demanded. On occasion, families or entire tribal groups were brought into violent conflict.

Wealth was measured in dentalium shell money and redheaded woodpecker scalps, but the most prestigious treasure was a complete dance costume for one of the traditional dance-feasts. The earliest among these were unusual costumes of white deerskin, elaborate headdresses and large obsidian ceremonial blades which the dancers wore or carried. Owners of such garments — which were usually inherited — were greatly respected as members of an important household or family unit. They often became leaders of the white deerskin

The Indian woman in younger years a beautiful maiden, now with a saddened smile creeping across the deep wrinkles of the dark-skinned face, cried out while her stubby fingers twisted about her kerchief: "Too bad white man find this place!" She paused and looked wistfully upstream... "For long time no one found us. Oh, too bad!"

(Humboldt Times, November 16, 1958 from an observation circa 1916)

dance or other ceremonials. Marriage was arranged by purchase, and men had as many wives as they could afford.

Religion played a significant role in daily life, and tribal doctors were nearly always women who received instructions in their craft directly from the spirits of departed ancestors. A distinctive religious practice held in autumn and spring was the rite of world renewal. This ceremony and dance at specific traditional spots along the Klamath River and its tributaries was held to insure bountiful crops and an abundance of deer and salmon. It was also celebrated to prevent earthquakes, illness, floods — even the destruction of the universe. The rite of world renewal was a joyous occasion and was widely attended. Singing, dancing, and feasting went on for days.

Native Americans of the Klamath River region were highly accomplished in crafts. Living in houses of hand-adzed redwood planks, they used cleverly-worked bone and horn implements to create ornate, intricate, and functional basketry. Clothing made of deer and other animal skins was loose-fitting but well-tailored. Feathers and seed pods, as well as abalone and other shells, were used in jewelry-making. Hunting implements included the bow and arrow, the sling, and the deersnare. Fishermen employed hooks, spears, traps, and nets. Throughout the area river travel was common in unique dugout canoes made of redwood or cedar.

Salmon and various shellfish, along with deer and elk, were the principle sources of protein. Pinenuts, hazelnuts, grass seeds, bulbs, and many varieties of berries joined the all-important acorn to complete a nutritious and palatable menu.

The initial contact with the white race probably came from the sea — coastal explorers in search of new sources of fur. It has been suggested that Sir Francis Drake may have been first to set foot in the region in 1579. Nearly 200 years later, the Spanish explorer Bruno de Heceta found iron knives already in use by the local Indians. Then, in 1828, Jedediah Smith led an overland party of 20 men with 300 horses and mules into this new territory. Exploration quickly burgeoned into migration.

The new settlers were heavy-handed and merciless in their dealings with the land and its original inhabitants. They relentlessly pushed back the forests for their homesteads and wastefully depleted wildlife resources. Conflict between the settlers and Indians was inevitable and ultimately brutal. The Indians did not understand the white men's thirst for additional land or their lack of personal honor. Almost all the settlers despised a race they considered inferior There were many provocations and retaliations. Skirmishes involving one or more settlers and the "diggers" (a derogatory term for Indians) resulted in punitive raids by vigilantes, sometimes in combination with the local militia.

As the tide of settlers increased, so did their covetousness. One local newspaper editorialized:

(page opposite) Distribution of Indian tribal (family) groups in northwestern California at the time of white discovery. Although Emma B. Freeman distinguished only two groups, the Hoopa (Hupa) and Klamath (Yurok and Karok), several other tribal groups were present in the area.

128

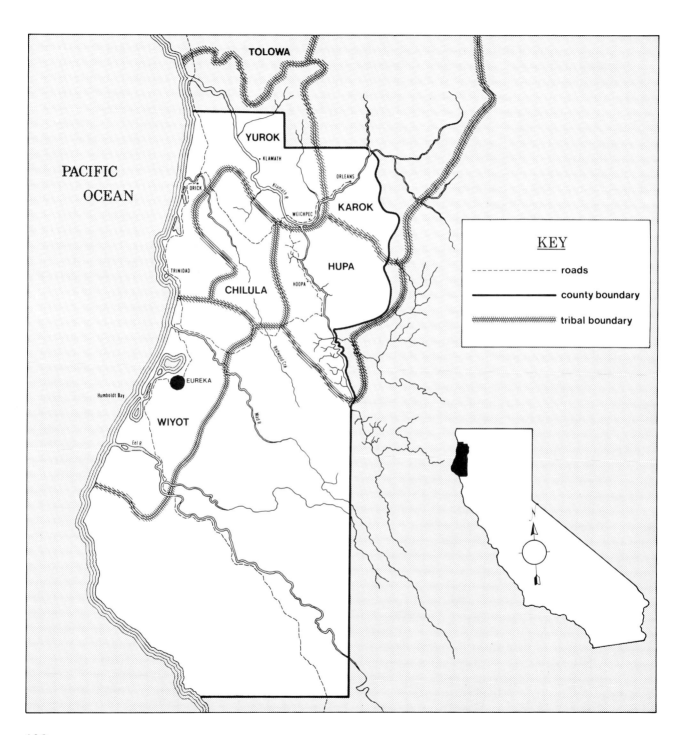

PACIFIC
OCEAN

TOLOWA

YUROK

KLAMATH

ORLEANS

ORICK

Klamath R

WEICHPEC

KAROK

HUPA

TRINIDAD

HOOPA

CHILULA

Redwood Cr.

Humboldt Bay

EUREKA

Mad R

WIYOT

Eel R

129

*It is a shame and a disgrace . . . that some of the best sections of our country must be placed beyond the reach of the hardy frontiersman by a few bands of miserable diggers.*

**(Humboldt Times, February 4, 1860)**

With mounting depredations and abuses, Colonel Francis J. Lippitt, Commander of the Humboldt Military District, recorded:

*No Indian can show his head anywhere without being shot down like a wild beast. The women and children even are considered good game . . .*

**(U.S. Dept. of War. War of the Rebellion, Part 1, 1880-01)**

The *San Francisco Bulletin,* in 1856, added:

*Some of the agents and nearly all of the employees, we are informed on one of the reservations at least, are daily and nightly engaged in kidnapping the younger portion of the females, for the vilest of purpose. The wives and daughters of the defenseless diggers are prostituted before the very eyes of their husbands and fathers, by these civilized monsters, and they dare not resent the insult, or even complain of the hideous outrage.*

**(San Francisco Bulletin, Sept. 13, 1856)**

The illegal kidnapping of Indian children, coupled with the quasi-legal indenture laws of Humboldt County, led to a brisk trafficking of Indian children into agricultural areas throughout California.

In 1860, little more than a month after the above editorial in the *Humboldt Times,* a premeditated massacre occurred on Indian Island, a spit of land in Humboldt Bay adjacent to Eureka. Nearly 200 peaceful Indians were murdered on the Island and at nearby sites. The vast majority of the victims were women and children.

A letter to the *San Francisco Bulletin* by a reputed eyewitness reported:

*Amidst the wailing of mutilated infants, the cries of children, the shrieks and groans of mothers in death, the savage blows are given, cutting through bone and brain. The cries for mercy are met by joke and libidinous remark while the bloody ax descends with unpitying stroke, again and again, the hatchet and knife finishing what the ax left undone.*

**(San Francisco Bulletin, March 13, 1860)**

The slaughter was condemned by a majority of the white citizens, including writer and journalist Bret Harte, who was present as a reporter for the *Northern Californian.* But the perpetrators were never punished. Less violent practices of discrimination and racial slur continued, and the terms "digger" or "savage" were used at all levels of white society. The Indian was stereotyped as thieving, lazy, treacherous, and childlike, and every aspect of Indian life was subjected to ridicule. The *Blue Lake Advocate,* which had a particularly malignant attitude toward the Indians, commented:

*It is learned that in about a week a great "Redskin dance" will occur at the Hoopa reservation which will last several weeks. This sort of dance is particularly enjoyed by the aborigines who are the only participants. The Indians have a great jollification during these dances. An ordinary white man who might happen to see them during such a festival would most likely get sick from laughter.*

**(Blue Lake Advocate, August 26, 1893)**

Even whites who were favorably disposed to the Indians condescendingly referred to those of them having a "capacity" to become proper and useful, as "civilized" Indians. Repressive measures continued, and at times incarceration of Indians in reservations like so many cattle seemed to be the ultimate goal of government policy. Throughout this repression, discrimination, and outright slaughter, the white man's diseases, his alcohol, and his enforcement of his own morality added to the ever-greater toll of Indian lives.

By the close of the Nineteenth Century, the white man of Northwestern California had virtually annihilated the Indians and their culture. He had settled the frontier, erected his churches, and surrounded his brightly painted houses with white picket fences. With the hardships and conflict of the frontier behind him, he now sought extensive social intercourse. Many fraternal groups were instituted to fill this need.

One of these white brotherhoods ironically became known as the "Improved Order of Redmen." This whites-only group professed its unity with the noble concepts and romantic ideals of man's interaction with the wilderness. To these latter-day "Redmen," the outdoors was a "wilderness of Hiawatha," and the movement seized the imagination of young men throughout the West. The Eureka branch of Redmen once boasted more than 700 members.

Structured in a wildly eclectic fashion, the brotherhood borrowed Indian principles at whim. Each "Wigwam" held its "Pow-wows," elected its "Chiefs," fined its "Braves," and collected their "Wampum." The Eureka Wigwam was of the Order of the Hupa, while Crescent City's, 70 miles to the North, was known by the exotic name Too-Toot-Ne. One notice in a local newspaper, under the headline *"Hupa Tribe Installs Chiefs,"* detailed the new holders of offices of *"Great Sachem," "Sannap Prophet," "Keeper of the Wampum," "First Warrior,"* and the like.

It is worth contrasting the Indian rite of world renewal with the Tenth Anniversary of the Hupa Tribe of Redmen:

*. . . spectacular entertainment was given the people of Eureka last nite by members of Hupa tribe of Redmen when a prairie schooner driven by palefaces down "F" St. at a rapid pace was overtaken by mounted warriors and the crowd*

*led by a band made their way to the pavilion where an all night dance had been announced. Until 10 o'clock the floor was utilized by the dancers and then for an hour the Redmen held forth in Indian dances. Three were given, the Fire dance, the Medicine dance, and the Brush dance . . . a score of warriors in full regalia trailed in single file and formed in a circle. They began in a low chant which gradually increased in fervor until the pavilion resounded with their cries, then sank to a whisper again. This was repeated over and over again, each repetition having a meaning of its own. While the chanting was in progress the savages kept up a pounding, in one dance with their knees and in the last dance with their feet. In the center by the fire was the leader or chief, bearing in his arms a little papoose . . . For the occasion the pavilion had been artistically decorated . . . particularly attractive, a number of genuine teepees . . . In front of them was placed the band and in the very forefront was a pair of live bears . . . their plaintive cries seemed particularly appropriate as the dancing Redmen circled about their dying campfire in the center of the building.*

**(Humboldt Times, June 22, 1913)**

The Indian civilization had been suppressed. When it resurfaced as a mystique, it had become a hash of misunderstood and misapplied symbols. Yet, it was at exactly this time, the period shortly before World War I, that Emma Freeman plunged into her series of idealized portraits of Northern California's Indians.

# Selected References

## Books

Arnold, Mary Ellicott and Mabel Reed. *In the Land of the Grasshopper Song; A story of two girls in Indian country in 1908-09.* New York: Vantage Press; 1957.

A charming account of two young white ladies among the Native Americans of the upper Klamath River region.

Bernier, R. L. Edition Deluxe *California's Magazine.* 2 vols. San Francisco: California's Magazine Company; 1916.

An excellent overview of the status of the fine arts in California at the time of the Panama-Pacific International Exposition.

Bledsoe, A. J. *Indian Wars of the Northwest.* San Francisco: Bacon & Company; 1885.

Written from the settlers' point of view; includes Humboldt and Del Norte counties.

Board of Supervisors of Del Norte County. *Del Norte County, California; and adjacent territory.* n.p.,n.d.

A typical example of the ubiquitous promotional literature of the 1916 period; illustrated.

Coke, Van Deren. *The Painter and the Photograph; from Delacroix to Warhol.* Albuquerque: University of New Mexico Press; 1972.

Coy, Owen C. Ph.D. *The Humboldt Bay Region 1850-1875: A study in the American Colonization of California.* Los Angeles: The California State Historical Association; 1929.

A scholarly account of the development of the Humboldt County region.

Curtis, Edward S. *The North American Indians.* vol. 13. Cambridge: the University Press; 1921.

Contains fine documentary images of the Yurok, Tolowa and Hupa peoples during the 1917 period.

Doty, Robert. *Photo-Secession, Photography as a Fine Art.* New York: The George Eastman House; 1960.

Goddard, Pliny Earle. *Life and Culture of the Hupa.* Berkeley: University of California Press; 1903.

Heizer, Robert F. and Alan J. Almquist. *The Other Californians.* Berkeley: University of California Press; 1971.

This work clearly describes the prejudices and oppression of the minorities by the white settlers.

Heizer, Robert F. and John E. Mills. *The Four Ages of Tsurai.* Berkeley: University of California Press; 1952.

A historical profile of a northcoast Indian village.

Humboldt County Chamber of Commerce. *Souvenir of Humboldt County, California.* Eureka: the Times Publishing Company; n.d.

An illustrated promotional booklet extolling the benefits of the Humboldt County region.

Irvine, Leigh Hadley. *History of Humboldt County, California.* Los Angeles: Historical Record Company; 1915.

Kroeber, A. L. *Handbook of the Indians of California.* Washington: Government Printing Office; 1925.

Mann, Margery and Anne Noggle. *Women of Photography: An Historical Survey.* San Francisco: San Francisco Museum of Art; 1975.

A catalogue to an exhibition of an historical survey of 50 women photographers.

Palmquist, Peter E. *Fine California Views: The photographs of A. W. Ericson.* Eureka: Interface California Corporation; 1975.

The documentary photographs of the Humboldt County region taken by Ericson during the 1885-1925 period.

Thompson, Mrs. Lucy. *To the American Indian.* Eureka: the Cummins Print Shop; 1916.

An interesting work about the customs of the Yurok Indian culture written by a Yurok of high birth.

Thornbury, D.L. *California's Redwood Wonderland: Humboldt County.* San Francisco: Sunset Press; 1923.

A chatty and informative account of the Humboldt County region as seen from a motor car excursion.

*Articles*

Borcoman, James. "Purism versus Pictorialism; the 135 years war." *Artscanada* (An Inquiry into the Asthetics of Photography issue) December, 1974.

*Newspapers*

Eureka, California, *Humboldt Standard.* 1884-1967.

Eureka, California, *Humboldt Times.* 1854-1967.

**PHOTO CREDITS:**

62, Eureka-Humboldt Library; 125, Clarke Memorial Museum; 8, 46, 50, 51, 85, 89, 97, 103, Courtesy of the Edward E. Ayer Collection, The Newberry Library, Chicago; 39, 47, Indian Action Library; cover, 19, 43, 44, 56, 75, 77, 79, 81, 83, 91, 93, 95, 99, California State Library, California Collection; 27, 30, 40, 101, 105, Allan R. Carlson; 48, 53, 55, 69, Bertha Stevens Chamley; 87, Gertrude Clausen; 29 Henry R. Frank.